Many Options *Few* Easy
Controlling School Spending

Ralph P. Kerr, Ed.D

Many Options Few Easy
Controlling School Spending
by Ralph P. Kerr, Ed.D

Printed in the United States of America

ISBN 9781615797172

www.xulonpress.com

TABLE OF CONTENTS

Dedication

This book is dedicated to my nine grandchildren all of whom have been impacted to one degree or another by the education they have received in school. Children like these cause me to want to continue my efforts to make quality education for all children a high priority in my life and a Constitutional right I want to help preserve.

Endorsements

" *A*s a new school board member, I found Dr. Kerr's book particularly helpful in seeking ways for our school district to spend public funds wisely, efficiently and equitably.

School board members in New York State and elsewhere face a daunting challenge in finding and preserving the financial resources we need to deliver the kind of education the public wants and expects.

The book continues to be a valued resource to me in my current duties as a school board member and chairperson of our district's Audit Committee."

> Doug Crandall,
> School Board Member
> Cuba-Rushford Central School District,
> Cuba, New York

"Many and varied are the choices facing administrators of the schools of the 21st century. The complexity of these matters gets more challenging as the needs grow in the public's school. Being the case, the leaders of tomorrow's schools will be greatly assisted by the compendium of tried and true solutions examined in this book.

Dr. Kerr has done an outstanding job of mixing the practical, pragmatic and the theoretical solutions, to common issues and questions facing the school administrator. This book is surely destined to become a mainstay reference in the libraries of all administrators, now and in the future."

John Delaney,
Retired School Superintendent
Trumansburg Central School District
Trumansburg, New York

Introduction

There are stark financial realities bombarding us from various sources throughout our nation. Most elected leaders; quasi government organizations and leaders of our unions fail to see the realities and instead appear to be living in a dream world.

Instead of forcing state and local officials to work with the hand dealt to them by the current financial realities, the Federal government in 2009 stepped in and passed the American Recovery and Reinvestment Act at a cost of $787 billion.

For public education this meant an influx of $44 billion in 2009 and the promise of an additional $49 billion in 2010. U.S. Secretary of Education Arne Duncan indicated "… the distribution of these funds was intended to save and create jobs and improve education in the short term."

Reportedly the stimulus plan has saved or created 250,000 jobs nationally in education. In California, the stimulus was credited with saving or creating 62,000 jobs in public schools and state universities. Utah reported saving about 2,600 teaching jobs.

The author of this book, a 30 year veteran of public education, maintains that what the intervention of the Federal government actually did was postpone the inevitable. All government entities and particularly public education must realize sooner or later that despite good intentions and desires, the taxpaying public cannot continue to increase funding for education as it has in the past. To his credit Education Secretary Duncan did say, "These are one-time funds, and state and school officials need to find the best way to stretch every dollar and spend the money in ways that protect and support children without carrying continuing costs."

This book, **Many Options Few Easy Controlling School Spending** contains many options, over 100 in fact, that are available to school administrators, board of education members and others interested in preserving public education as they wrestle with the daunting task of controlling school spending. Very few of these options are easy ones to select; therefore they turn out to be very hard choices. Hard choices however that must be made if taxpayer support for public education is to continue into the future.

CHAPTER ONE

Reality in a Dream World

Here is the reality of the current economic state of our country:

- The unemployment rate sits near 10 percent.

This unemployment rate is the highest since June 1983. The latest monthly net total loss of jobs was 263,000. If laid-off workers who have settled for part-time work or have given up looking for new jobs are included, the unemployment rate is at 17 percent, the highest on record since 1994. In many states the only areas where employment has increased in any significant measure is in the areas of health care and government services, including education.

- The stock market's Dow Jones Industrial Average lost another 203 points in one day.

While the stock market has recovered some of its earlier dramatic loses individual private pension savings continue to show huge declines. People who had anticipated retirement in the near future are reviewing those plans with the thought of continuing to work for the foreseeable future.

- According to an Adweek Media/Harris Poll, seventy-nine percent of Americans have reduced their spending in the last twelve months.

The impact of this reduction in spending can be seen during visits to shopping malls, restaurants and particularly in big ticket item stores like automobile dealerships.

- Foreclosures on homes have risen substantially. One in eight mortgages is currently in foreclosure or default.
- No cost of living increase will be given to Social Security recipients in 2010.
- In September 2009 the Federal Government faced a $1.6 trillion deficit. It faces a cumulative 10 year deficit of about $9 trillion. That's $30,000 for each man, woman and child in the United States.
- According to the Government Accountability Office, state and local governments were expected to face an operating deficit of $131 billion in 2009 and $181 billion in 2010.
- The Center on Budget, Policies and Priorities reports that 48 of 50 states have already experienced budget shortfalls.
- Due to a major budget crisis in 2009, including a $26 billion budget gap, the State of California was forced to issue IOU's instead of having the cash to pay its' bills.

- In the midst of the recent budget crisis California slashed aid to school districts again. This is the fourth time since 2008. The $6 billion reduction in July 2009 was part of the agreement to close the overall budget gap.

According to the California Teachers Association, more than 17,000 teachers have been laid off in an effort to close the budget gap. The State has postponed the adoption of new textbooks until at least the 2013-14 academic year.

- The State of Georgia had a $900 million deficit within three months of adopting its latest budget. Delaware and Georgia are cutting teachers pay through unpaid furlough days.
- The most recent North Carolina state budget reduced state aid to schools by $400 million. The state education department in North Carolina plans to eliminate 100 of the 475 agency's positions over the next two years.
- In Idaho, 18 of the state's 115 school districts recently declared a "financial emergency" under state law, allowing them to reopen collective bargaining agreements with teachers' unions.
- The Governor of Virginia announced his state's $77 billion budget will have to be reduced by another $1.5 billion to balance the budget.
- Officials in Maine are trying to determine how to deal with a state budget shortfall between $60 and $100 million.
- To deal with dwindling cash, Illinois and New Jersey delayed state aid payments to school districts for services such as transportation, special education and bilingual programs.

- Districts in Minnesota have been forced to borrow from banks due to delays in state aid payments by the State.
- Pennsylvania was over three months late in adopting its 2009-10 State budget wreaking havoc throughout the state.
- New York State Comptroller Tom DiNapoli issued a report indicating that if current trends continue his state runs the risk of a $38 billion spending gap through State Fiscal Year 2012-13.

Most elected leaders, quasi government organizations and leaders of our unions fail to see the reality of our current economic situation.

Despite these stark financial realities throughout our nation, most elected leaders, quasi government organizations and leaders of our unions fail to see the realities and instead appear to be living in a dream world.

Out of necessity the leaders of many of our national charitable organizations have bravely faced the world of reality we are currently living in. Despite the fact that charitable spending has grown faster than the national economy for the last 20 years these leaders have exercised responsible, though heart wrenching leadership behaviors. According to a survey of the 1000 members of the Evangelical Council for Financial Accountability the Council found that:

- 41 percent had frozen or delayed salary increases
- 38 percent had frozen or reduced hiring
- 19 percent had laid off staff
- 11 percent had cut salaries
- 53 percent had cut travel and conference expenses

In response to the layoff of 40 people as part of a 12 percent budget reduction, caused by a $2.8 million deficit, one charitable organization president said, "We know if we do not make up this shortfall, we will be forced to make even more cuts."

This is quite a different response than from elected leaders, quasi government organization, school boards and leaders of our labor unions. Fortunately there are some indications that some of these leaders are beginning to hear the message tax payers are giving.

After the 2 – 1 resounding rejection of a series of ballot measures by voters of California that would have closed a $21.3 billion budget gap Governor Arnold Schwarzenegger said, "I think the message was clear from people. Go all out and make those cuts and live within your means."

Instead of forcing state and local officials to work with the hand dealt to them by the financial realities the Federal government in 2009 stepped in and passed the American Recovery and Reinvestment Act at a cost of $890 billion.

For schools this meant an influx of $44 billion in 2009 and the promise of an additional $49 billion in 2010. U.S. Secretary of Education Arne Duncan indicated that "… the distribution of these funds was intended to save and create jobs and improve education in the short term." To his credit Secretary Duncan went on to say, "These are one-time funds, and state and school officials need to find the best way to stretch every dollar and spend the money in ways that protect and support children without carrying continuing costs."

As well intentioned as this influx of money may have been, the infusion of these one-time funds really just postponed the inevitable. All government entities and particularly public education must realize sooner or later that despite good intentions and desires, the taxpaying public cannot continue to increase funding for education as it has in the past, nor can the State or Federal government.

Officials at the New York State School Boards Association referred to the stimulus money this way, "Federal stimulus funding has been described as fiscal anesthesia...and anesthesia wears off. Were it not for this ultimate 'one shot,' our schools would be facing wholesale cuts in programs, services and staffing."

New York State Governor David Paterson said, "Federal stimulus funding provided the state with a soft landing as it transitions to a new fiscal reality, but much more needs to be done to get our fiscal house in order."

Whether the stimulus money is viewed as "fiscal anesthesia" or a "soft landing" it certainly is a "one time fund." Rather than commit to help the States get their fiscal houses in order leaders of various State organizations had these responses.

Timothy G. Kremer, Executive Director of New York State School Boards Association.

"No cuts from current level funding!"

"We cannot escape the fact that building a world class education system requires a great teacher in the classroom, a strong leadership team in every district and, yes, financial resources. At the very least, the state must hold school districts harmless in next year's state budget, with no cuts from current year funding levels. Let's not make our children the brunt of those 'horrible economic choices' the governor referenced in his speech."

Kremer continued, "We applaud the governor's call for relief from burdensome state mandates, though we have serious concerns about imposing a tax cap at a time when the governor has proposed dramatic cuts in state aid to education. Such a move would leave schools with no alternative but to drastically cut programs and people. That would undoubtedly impact students and the opportunities provided them in our public schools."

It's no wonder the Executive Director of NYSSBA responds this way when nearly two thirds of the respondents in an online poll of school board members in the State said they believe the State budget did not provide adequate aid to their school district.

Dr. Thomas L. Rogers, former Executive Director of the New York State Council of School Superintendents.

"Advocating for an increase of $879 million."

"We will be advocating for a funding level like that recommended by our state Board of Regents, an increase of $879 million. That would come closer to what is needed to maintain our progress in student achievement in the state. Cutting school aid, eliminating STAR rebates and shifting preschool special education costs to schools would increase school property tax pressures. We appreciate the mandate relief proposals the governor has made, but we hope that he and the legislators will consider more."

"The economic crisis is severe but we cannot and do not accept this devastating $2.5 billion School-Aid cut as inevitable."

New York State United Teachers (NYSUT) is the state's largest union representing more than 600,000 classroom teachers and other school employees, faculty and other professionals at the state's community colleges, State University of New York and City University of New York, and other education and health professionals. NYSUT President Richard C. Iannuzzi, said this, "New York State United Teachers, while recognizing that the darkening economy requires difficult decisions, Gov. Paterson's proposed state education budget would ask students to shoulder the burden of the state's economic crisis, resulting in increased class sizes, cuts in academic services and reduced access to the states community colleges at a time when it's needed most. Although we respect the governor's efforts to craft a budget in these trying times this spending proposal raises deep concerns about its impact on public education. The economic crisis is severe but we cannot and do not accept this devastating $2.5 billion School-Aid cut as inevitable."

Iannuzzi continued, "We give the governor credit for including new sources of revenue but they don't begin to go far enough to enable the state to meet its obligations to our students. Deep cuts to education unfairly burden children instead of asking the wealthiest to shoulder their fair share to a more progressive income tax. These deep cuts would represent a huge disinvestment in New York State at a time when equity and economic recovery depend on quality public education."

In some cases actions of those living in the "dream world," particularly at a local level are speaking even louder than the rhetoric of organizational leaders. For example in Ohio while many Ohioans are seeing their paychecks frozen, cut or taken away, pay raises for teachers top 5 percent in some districts once all automatic pay bumps are included. John Herrington of the Educate Worthington organization is helping to lead a growing debate in Ohio not only about whether teachers should take pay concessions in the short term, but if the school district's salary structures are sustainable in the future. His conclusion, "They are not!"

Present school employee's salary structures are not sustainable in the future.

The Gates-Chili Central School District in suburban Rochester, NY announced a four year agreement in September 2009 in which teachers will receive salary increases of 3 percent, 3.75 percent, 3.95 percent and 3.95 in the final year. In exchange for these significant salary increases totaling 14.65 percent over four years, teachers agreed to **begin** contributing towards their health insurance premiums. The rate of contribution moves from 0 percent in the first year to 5 percent, 7 percent and 10 percent in year four. The net cost to the district for the total package will be about 3 percent each year. In commenting on the contract the teachers union President said, "Teachers are aware of the tough economic times and are overwhelmingly in support of the new contract." Even more outlandish is the comment of the Superintendent. He stated, "This contract captures the awareness of the economic times. It is an example of win-win negotiations. It was fair to both parties."

One wonders how fair the average taxpayer of the district feels the contract settlement is to them, particularly in light of the fact that the average wage and salary increase for non-government employees in the 12 month period ending June 2009 was 1.8 percent, according to the U.S. Bureau of Labor Statistics. Raises in 2010 are not expected to top 2 percent, according to federal estimates. Yet teachers are receiving increases of 3 to 5 percent.

Living in a "dream world" like this causes strong reactions from many corners of our society. George F. Will a columnist for Newsweek magazine opined in the March 23, 2009 edition, "For decades, state legislatures, encouraged by teacher unions, have embraced the theory that schools' cognitive outputs were a function of financial inputs. The theory was: As with soybeans, so with education – if you want more, increase subsidies." In the March 9, 2009 edition of the same magazine Warren Buffett said, "Weaning these entities from the public teat will be a political challenge. They won't leave willingly."

Even Albert Shanker, former President, American Federation of Teachers' said, "It's time to admit that public education operates like a planned economy, a bureaucratic system in which everybody's role is spelled out in advance and there are few incentives for innovation and productivity. It's no surprise that our school system doesn't improve."

What is really alarming is when one looks at the average life span of a country and begins to think about where we are as a country in our life span. In their book, <u>Armageddon, Oil and Terror</u>, John Walvoord and Mark Hitchcock (Tyndale House Publishers, 2007) take an historical look at the life span of countries. Each of the nations studied progressed through the following sequence: from bondage to spiritual faith; from spiritual faith to great courage; from courage to liberty; from liberty to abundance; from abundance to complacency; from complacency to apathy; from apathy to dependence; and from dependency back to bondage."

Instead of reality prevailing, the "dream world" continues. The critical question however is how long can the "dream world" continue before things totally collapse and the collapse takes our country and our increasing dependency down with it?

Instead, in my earlier book, **The Sin of Apathy**, (Xulon Press, 2009) I reviewed the widespread apathy among people as it relates to the public school systems of our nation. Instead of getting actively involved in our schools I demonstrated with example after example how the public has allowed the "enemies" of public education to virtually take over the system. The enemies documented include the teacher unions, school boards, school board associations, our court systems and the judges and finally school administrators.

My growing concern now is that while apathy continues among the general public a growing dose of dependency is being dispensed by the federal government in terms of stimulus money, automobile company bailouts, bank and insurance company takeovers, along with student loans. Can bondage as Walvoord and Hitchcock describe it be far behind?

The purpose of this book is to wrestle with two important questions. These are:

1) **How do school districts balance taxpayer affordability with the program and financial needs of the district?**
2) **If the school board and administrators determine that the current program and financial needs of the district out strip the ability of the taxpayers to pay what steps can be taken to reduce the program and financial needs of the district?**

Let's deal with question #1 first. How do school districts balance taxpayer affordability with the program and financial needs of the district?

There are several key words in this question. Let's look at them. *Taxpayer Affordability.*

Who decides what taxpayers can afford? Can they afford more but are unwilling to pay? Do taxpayers have other priorities for their money and should they? These are difficult questions with no easy answers, at least not answers that will satisfy everyone.

School districts receive its funds from primarily three sources, the Federal Government, State Government and local taxpayers. Do you notice any common thread among these three sources? Let me ask the question another way.

Does the federal government have any money of its own? No, not unless you count the US mint where the government actually makes the money the federal government uses. So the real answer to the question does the federal government have any money of its own is "No!" Does the state government have any money of its own? "No!"

Both the federal and state governments do have money which they collect through taxes and fees. Both levels of government also spend significant money on education. Total dollars spent annually nationwide amounts to over $500 billion. The source of most of the money is the taxpayer in our country or in our states, in other words, you and me. Who by the way are the same people who are considered the local taxpayers.

In recent years most school districts have received increased funds from the federal government, huge increases in state aid from the state, and yet have continued to ask local taxpayers to increase the amount of money they are paying for their schools.

It is difficult to arbitrarily say what the right amount of money is that the district should receive. It does seem to me however that in many cases school districts have hardly taken into consideration the major increases they have received from the federal and state government when they decide on the increases they are going to propose to the local taxpayer. The interesting part of this situation however is that district voters, in most districts have an opportunity to vote on the school budget and while they complain loudly about the increases they still vote for the budget. Frankly, to my dismay voters continue to support the increased budgets at a record pace.

Education costs will continue to escalate until local voters say "NO" to the budgets.

School budgets will continue to increase at this record pace if taxpayers fail to give school board members an indication, at least in a demonstrative way, that they are concerned about these increases and will not support them in the voting booth. I believe voters will begin sending this message very clearly, very soon. In other words I predict that beginning with the 2011-2012 school year, if not sooner, we will see record numbers of school budgets fail for lack of voter support UNLESS school board members and district administrators step up and make the difficult but necessary financial reductions and control school spending.

The other key words in the earlier statement are: *Program and Financial Needs.* In a school setting how does one determine the difference between wants and needs? It may be easy to define basic building maintenance, reading supplies, textbooks and the like, as needs in the school. It may not be as easy to make the case to support financially, staff development, public relations, elementary guidance or to answer such questions as: "At what grade level do we begin to teach foreign language?" So, are these latter items wants or needs?

Frequently today when a conversation turns to the economy the ever increasing cost of financing schools inevitably crops up. Of particular concern is the annual increase of local property taxes. In school districts anywhere from 10% to 92% of the total costs of financing schools comes from the local property tax. The actual percentage is determined by the property and personal wealth of the local taxpayers.

In many recent years when the inflation rate nationally hovered around 3% school districts increased the local property tax by more than double the inflation rate. The mind set of many people in education, particularly those who have responsibility for developing budgets seems to be that the ability of the taxpayer to pay the bill should not be a factor taken into consideration. The standard line is, "The students of the district need these things for their education, so despite the costs the taxpayers have an obligation to provide them." Teachers unions in particular are notorious for taking this position.

It seems to me the desire to balance taxpayer's affordability with the financial needs of a school should be paramount. Unfortunately a school board candidate who thinks this way should be prepared for opposition from every union affiliated with the schools, most administrators and even fellow board members. The arguments against this point of view can become sentimental, "Shouldn't we do all we can for the children?" or downright demanding and personal. "You can't control costs on the backs of the teachers and others who have served the children of this district so faithfully for all these years." People who continue to hold this viewpoint, given the stark reality of the current world we live in, are living in a "dream world."

These few paragraphs demonstrate clearly the difficulty of balancing taxpayer affordability with the program and financial needs of the school. This work however is part of the important tasks of the school superintendent and board members and needs to be done.

The second, and for the purposes of this book the most important question is: If the school board and administrators determine that the current program and financial needs of the district out strip the ability of the taxpayers to pay, what steps can be taken to reduce the program and financial needs of the district?

School budget downsizing can mean making painful decisions.

The assumptions made in regard to all of the discussion through the remainder of this book is that along with the inability of local taxpayers to pay more, the federal stimulus money will be discontinued and, that out of necessity, state aid for education will be significantly reduced in the coming years. School budget downsizing can mean making painful decisions about program elimination and staff layoffs. When the graceful options are exhausted, what can be done? Like pruning an orchard, the downsizing of school budgets can be used to some advantage—discovering and reducing programs of limited benefit, making instructional programs more focused and more defensible, gathering detailed information about the district staff's effort, and tapping into staff ideas for cost-savings.

Preparation is the best approach to school budget downsizing. With an ongoing program of self-examination a district may not have to experience the wholesale layoffs, unattended school grounds, and dark buildings that may be imagined. Proper district preparation, planning and timely action, in the form of pruning can turn a dreaded experience into a positive outcome. A school district designed for the future that can offer an exemplary educational program that taxpayers can and will support financially.

CHAPTER TWO

Magnitude of the Financial Challenge

Here are two examples that illustrate the magnitude of the current problem if substantial reductions in state aid occur and known future cost increases are not addressed in a timely manner. These illustrations are followed by a detailed explanation of the components of the examples utilized.

Example 1, School district with a $21 million budget.

Proposed State Aid reduction (4%)		$500,000
Possible Increases		
1) Current Salaries	$8,500,000	
Contract Increase 4.5%	380,000	380,000
2) Current Benefits	$4,400,000	
Anticipated Increase 10%	440,000	440,000

3) Assume nothing else increases, not a realistic assumption but made only to illustrate the magnitude of the issue if only Salaries and Benefits increase.

TOTAL ANTICIPATED STATE AID REDUCTION AND EXPENDITURE INCREASE $1,320,000

Example 1 illustrates the financial impact of a $500,000 State Aid reduction for a school district with an annual total budget of $21 million. The proposed State Aid reduction is $500,000 or approximately 4 percent of the budget. Given the fact that in some previous State Aid reductions, where the percentage was 10 percent, the percentage presented in this scenario is certainly not extreme or unrealistic.

In most districts labor union contracts are already in place and may stipulate wage increases of up to 4.5% or $380,000 as used in this example. Additionally employee benefit increases, including state pension assessments and health insurance, can easily add up to another 10%, in this case, $440,000.

As a result, if one totals the anticipated State Aid reduction along with the known salary and benefit increase the anticipated budget shortfall would be $1,320,000. This example does not include other normal increases such as Special Education costs, utilities, fuel, BOCES* Administrative costs and a possible Debt Service increase which could add substantially to the total.

(* In New York State BOCES, the Board of Cooperative Education Services provides a variety of services to local school districts on a cooperative basis with the assumption that these services can be provided cooperatively at a reduced cost. Other States refer to these agencies by such names as Intermediate Service Agency or Intermediate School District.)

Depending on the assessed value of the property in a district with a budget of this size, and assuming no reserve funds were used, a local property tax increase of between 20% and 40% could be necessary if no reductions were made in the proposed budget.

Example 2, School district with a $58 million budget.

Proposed State Aid reduction (4%)		$2,200,000
Possible increases		
1) Current Salaries	$25,500,000	
Contract Increases 3%	765,000	765,000
2) Current Benefits	$15,000,000	
Increase 10%	1,500,000	1,500,000
3) Assume nothing else increases		

TOTAL ANTICIPATED STATE AID REDUCTION AND EXPENDITURE INCREASE   **$4,465,000**

Example 2 illustrates the financial impact of a $2,200,000 State Aid reduction for a school district with an annual total budget of $58 million. The proposed State Aid reduction is $2,200,000 or approximately 4 percent of the budget. Given the fact that in some previous State Aid reductions, where the percentage was 10 percent, the percentage presented in this scenario is certainly not extreme or unrealistic.

In most districts union contracts are already in place and may stipulate wage increases of 3 percent or $765,000 as used in this example. Additionally employee benefit increases, including state pension assessments and health insurance, can easily add up to another 10%, in this case, $1,500,000.

As a result, if one totals the anticipated State Aid reduction along with the known salary and benefit increase the anticipated budget shortfall would be $4,465,000. This example again does not include other normal increases such as Special Education costs, utilities, fuel, BOCES Administrative costs and a possible Debt Service increase which could add substantially to the total.

Depending on the assessed value of the property in a district with a budget of this size, and assuming no reserve funds were used, a local property tax increase of between 15% and 20% could be necessary if no reductions were made in the proposed budget.

Although no other cost increases are reflected in the above examples it should be noted that realistically the items listed below will likely increase in all districts.

1) Special Education costs including increased share of Preschool Special Education – 15% share of costs
2) Utilities
3) Fuel
4) BOCES Administrative Costs
5) Increases in Debt Service

CHAPTER THREE

Common Approaches to Budget Reductions

What do administrators and Boards of Education do when they are faced with the necessity of budget reductions? Generally the first thing is to protest to the Governor and other State representatives about the State Aid reductions. While such protestations may have "saved the day" in the past I believe that in the coming years these protestations will be to no avail as the politicians will be forced to admit they simply have no more tricks in their "bag of tricks" to provide the money. They also will have realized that increasing fees or taxes simply will not be tolerated any longer by taxpayers. They will be forced at last to admit they don't have any more taxpayer money to give away. Most politicians are ultimately concerned about re-election. Fortunately more and more taxpayers and voters are rousing from their apathetic attitudes and telling the politicians, "No more taxes!" These words have now become more than a slogan. They are a sentiment and mandate being voiced by most taxpayers.

So, once the administrators and Board members realize protesting the reductions to the Governor and State representatives will be to no avail they must come up with another strategy. Some districts will begin to actively involve their communities in the conversation by asking residents to choose which of the following items they would be willing to have the Board eliminate or reduce: Conferences, Equipment, Supplies, Field Trips, Athletics, Faculty or Staff. Generally the least favored item to eliminate or reduce is Faculty or Staff. There are significant fallacies with this approach. First, most responders have no idea how much money can actually be saved by eliminating or reducing any of these items. In the examples in the previous chapter where the budget shortfall ranges from $1.3 to $4.5 million the only item listed that has even the slightest potential to meet the shortfall is reducing faculty and/or staff. This will always be the least favored response by residents, faculty and staff.

Here is one example of the potential savings if **ALL** Conferences, Equipment, Field Trips, Athletics, Extra Curricular Programs and Supplies were eliminated.

Example 1 – School District - $21 million budget

Item	Potential Savings
Conferences	$ 16,000
Equipment	378,000
Field Trips	22,000
Athletics and Extra Curricular	260,000
Supplies	148,000
TOTAL SAVINGS	$824,000
REMAINING SHORTFALL	**$496,000**

Example 2 – School District - $58 million budget

Item	Potential Savings
Conferences	$ 40,000
Equipment	500,000
Field Trips	55,000
Athletics and Extra Curricular	590,000
Supplies	445,000
TOTAL SAVINGS	$1,630,000
REMAINING SHORTFALL	**$2,835,000**

Even if all these items listed were cut in the example districts shown, there would still be shortfalls of $496,000 and $2.8 million respectively. Obviously, cutting all these items is not likely to occur and even if the cuts did occur the remaining shortfall is huge. It should also be noted that of the five items listed in the above examples proposing to cut all Athletics in most districts would bring out the largest attendance ever seen at the next Board of Education meeting. At best a board might be able to reduce some money from each of these budget items but the end result would be hundreds of thousands of dollars in reductions would still need to be found elsewhere.

Put the "dream world" of the past behind and move into the "world of reality."

The next chapters of this book get to the heart of the matter of overcoming the sin of indulgence and outline many choices that could be considered, few of which are easy ones. Hard choices do need to be made and they need to be made soon. The following pages are filled with detailed descriptions of possible Budget Reductions and a brief description of Revenue Enhancers that districts might consider.

If you are a school Administrator or a Board of Education member I urge you to put the "dream world" of the past behind you and move into the new "world of reality." If you are a concerned citizen/taxpayer in your school district I urge you to begin to have a conversation now with your school Administrators and members of the Board of Education. The choices presented in the next chapters can serve as a discussion starter in your school district. They can also help make the extremely difficult decisions more thoughtful and constructive. I wish you well as you undertake the task of preserving public education.

The list of possible budget reductions is divided into three groups. **"Immediate Budget Reductions"** are reductions that a school board could authorize at a board meeting and the administration could have in place within 30 days. **"Intermediate Budget Reductions"** are reductions that a school board could authorize during the school year and expect to be in place no later than the beginning of the following school year. **"Long Term Budget Reductions"** are reductions that a board could have as long term goals to be accomplished over the next one to three years. Many of these items would require difficult negotiations with various bargaining units and real leadership within the entire community. Depending on the term of the existing contracts, one to three years or more may be needed to bring about these changes. Explanatory comments for each item are included after each listing.

These cost control solutions will vary in appropriateness depending on current district programs, community expectations and priorities.

The list of **Revenue Enhancers** is comprised of ways districts may be able to increase the revenue coming into the district's operating budget.

CHAPTER FOUR

Immediate Budget Reductions

The Immediate Budget Reductions are ones that a school board could authorize at a regular board meeting and in many cases the school administration could implement within 30 days, if not immediately.

1. Increase student prices for Breakfast and Lunch to assure the district does not subsidize the program.
2. Increase adult prices for the Lunch program to better reflect actual costs.
3. Reduce conference attendance
4. Reduce Staff Development, particularly out of district opportunities
5. Reduce or delay equipment purchases for at least one year
6. Reduce the number of field trips
7. Reduce supply purchases
8. Adjust "regular periodic maintenance" schedule of all buses

9. Lower heat in all buildings
10. Increase technology replacement cycle
11. Review future total district enrollment trends
12. Institute a Vacant Position Analysis
13. Eliminate Summer School
14. Eliminate Summer School Transportation
15. Review the number of students scheduled in Speech Therapy group sessions
16. Reduce legal counsel costs
17. Reduce Administrator/Teacher recruitment costs
18. Ask the Committee on Special Education to consider costs when developing student IEP's
19. Install photocopying monitoring devices on all copiers
20. Replace desktop printers with networked high-volume multifunctional copiers
21. Pull the plug on personal appliances
22. Look closely at dependents claimed by employees receiving health insurance
23. Review district health insurance premium payment amounts for retirees.
24. Increase lawn mowing cycle
25. Monitor overtime expenses
26. Combine sports teams transportation

Here is a detailed explanation of what is involved in the Immediate Budget Reductions with some specific examples of savings achieved by adopting these choices.

1. Increase student prices for Breakfast and Lunch to assure the district does not subsidize the program.

School districts are required to operate both a breakfast and lunch program for students. It is not the intent however that a school district will subsidize any deficit the food program incurs. In fact in some states it is against state regulations to do so. Districts should be aware of the financial condition of the food program and if a deficit does occur or is anticipated meal prices should be increased in a timely manner to cover the deficit.

Districts should also be aware of the impact of the price set for meals. For example, in one district the first full lunch for high school students cost $1.75. If students chose to purchase a second full lunch the cost was reduced to $.75. As a result students would pick the items they liked off each lunch and throw the rest away. Why should the exact same lunch cost $1.00 less for a student because it was the second lunch? Obviously there is no good reason for this differential. The practice did however contribute to the increasing food service deficit in this particular district. It also contributed to the amount of wasted food.

2. Increase adult prices for the Lunch program to better reflect actual costs.

While it is a convenience and helpful service to adults employed by a school district to make lunch available to them on site, school officials should be certain that the actual cost of providing this service is covered by the price being charged.

3. Reduce conference attendance

Most districts spend less than 1% of its total budget on conference attendance expense however it is still an area that should be reviewed as it can result in an expense reduction.

4. Reduce Staff Development, particularly out of district opportunities

All districts are required to have a professional development plan. The extent of the plan and its implementation is a local decision. Certainly decisions whether to offer the staff development in district or out of district is a local decision. Staff Development activities should be evaluated regularly to determine their effectiveness and impact on student achievement. In challenging times some reduction for a limited period of time and where the development is offered may be appropriate.

5. Reduce or delay equipment purchases for at least one year

Most planned equipment purchases such as lawn tractors, snow plowing equipment, even student and teacher desks and lab equipment could be reduced or at least delayed for one year without serious consequences.

6. Reduce the number of field trips

Field trip expense amounts to a small percentage of most school budgets. The purpose and educational value of all field trips should be reviewed on an annual basis. Often, over several years field trips become institutionalized and a trip which once may have been of substantial educational value is diminished in value.

7. Reduce supply purchases

Supplies often account for 7% - 8% of the total school budget. Even small reductions in this budget category can result in substantial savings. Often supplies not used one year are carried forward to the next. Supply budget requests are simply inflated from the previous year without consideration of actual needs or existing supplies.

8. Adjust "regular periodic maintenance" schedule of all buses.

Most school districts live by the myth that "regular periodic maintenance" of its bus fleet means buses must be inspected every 30 days or 1000 miles. This myth has been perpetuated by state bus inspectors who prefer this cycle, perhaps for self preservation and job security reasons. The law does call for "regular periodic maintenance" but the period of time that constitutes "regular" or "periodic" is not defined. As a result "regular periodic maintenance" could mean every 60 days or 2000 miles or even every 90 days or 3000 miles. Some districts have gone to a 60 day or 2000 miles inspection cycle and once the bus inspector made the adjustment the change has been successful and saved significant dollars. With over 28,000 buses in New York State alone, think of what the savings would be if more districts extended their inspection schedule.

9. Lower heat in all buildings.

A small decrease of one or two degrees in temperature in a school building can generate substantial savings in heating costs. Be sure to notify parents, staff and students of this change so they can dress appropriately. Lowering the heat has also been shown to be healthier for people in the building.

10. Increase technology replacement cycle.

Most districts have a detailed technology plan which includes annual purchases of new technology. These plans could probably be postponed for a year, given the financial circumstances districts find themselves in, without a major setback in the rolling out of the plan. Purchases made through a BOCES COSER, which are purchased on an installment plan, may present some challenges in postponing purchases.

Many districts have spent millions of dollars to bring the latest technology to their students and staff. Most districts also have an ongoing technology replacement plan which calls for technology to be updated on a specific cycle. This may amount to spending several hundreds of thousands of dollars or more each year. Simply letting the replacement cycle lag by a single year can bring enormous savings to a school budget.

11. Review future total district enrollment trends.

PreK-12 enrollment in public schools 2009-15 in the Northeast United States is projected to decline. For example in Pennsylvania the projected decrease is 1.7%. This follows a decrease of 4.1% in 2003-09. In New York State the projected decrease 2009-15 is 2.9%. This follows a decrease of 5.2% in 2003-09. As a result of these decreases local school districts should be examining its enrollment trends. Kelley D. Carey wrote an extremely informative article on this topic entitled, "Avoiding the Costly Mistakes" American School Board Journal, July 2009. Carey states, "Enrollment projections and mapping should be on a rolling five-year plan that is updated at the end of the third grading period each year. This allows you to incorporate demographic shifts and examine how new policies, such as changing promotion practices, will impact future enrollment."

Without a periodic review of future enrollment trends a district may hire additional personnel or make other expenditures that in the future may prove to have been unnecessary.

12. Institute a Vacant Position Analysis

All employee positions which are vacated, for whatever reason, whether on the Support Staff or Professional Staff should be subject to a Vacant Position Analysis. Some of the questions in need of answers are:

Is this position a state mandated position?
What does the position entail?
How does that position impact students?
Are there other ways to deliver the service for the
    students?

(A suggested form to be used during this process is included in the Appendix.)

13. Eliminate Summer School

Summer School is not a mandated program. Elimination of it has been done successfully in some districts. It is important that parents and students are informed as early as possible that there will be no summer school. This affords students the opportunity to utilize the regular school year instruction to its fullest.

One rural Upstate New York district had for many years offered a summer success program aimed at enhancing students' skills and English and Social Studies courses for ninth and tenth graders who needed the credit for grade promotion. Recently district officials discontinued the summer success program, leaving only the courses in English and Social Studies. This reduced program cost the district only $2400, a total savings of $31,100 annually.

14.   Eliminate Summer School Transportation

Obviously if summer school is eliminated so should summer school transportation. Even if summer school is not eliminated summer school transportation should be. Summer school transportation is not required by law and generally is offered as a "courtesy" to parents. One district projected it could save $70,000 by eliminating this "courtesy."

15.   Review the number of students scheduled in Speech Therapy group sessions

How many students should be assigned to a speech therapy group? Some expert speech therapists recommend five students is an acceptable and reasonable number. Districts who have reviewed the size of existing Speech Therapy groups often find two or three students are assigned to each group. Even if five students are assigned to a group seldom do all five students attend each session, for a variety of reasons.

16.   Reduce legal counsel costs

Attorney fees and other legal costs can be substantial. Hourly rates for attorneys with expertise in educational law range from $250 to $300. Rates are computed in quarter hour segments and recorded in logs. A district should periodically review the hourly rates it is being charged and consider requesting professional services proposals from a variety of law firms which specialize in education law. School boards should have a written policy regarding who is authorized to request information or advice from the districts' law firm. The district should review its legal bills to determine if requested "research" on legal questions is being done by an attorney or a paralegal. Once this has been determined the district should make certain that it is being billed at the proper rate of the party who is actually doing the "research" be it an attorney or paralegal. The Board should also review such practices as having an attorney on staff, on retainer or requiring that an attorney be in attendance at all school board meetings. Are these "conveniences" necessary?

17. Reduce Administrator/Teacher recruitment costs

During a time when districts are reducing the number of administrators and teachers due to budget considerations many continue to expend dollars to recruit administrators and teachers. This seems redundant.

18. Ask the Committee on Special Education to consider costs when developing student IEP's

Much care must be exercised here. The Committee of Special Education (CSE) is the only group charged with the responsibility of developing an Individualized Educational Plan (IEP) which is subsequently approved or disapproved by the Board of Education. The Committee should decide on the appropriate educational program for each student. The Committee should also be aware of the variation in costs of this appropriate educational program. For example, is an appropriate program offered "in district" less expensive than an "out of district" program? If so, the CSE should be recommending the "in district" program.

The district administration should also be regularly charting personnel employed or contracted to provide special education and related services to students with disabilities.

Data over time in the areas of classification, declassification, placement, student performance and fiscal matters should be studied. Additionally criteria for the use of 1:1 aides should be clear and the criteria should be adhered to. A system to track referrals for testing and CSE meetings by month and grade level should be in place. Such a monitoring system can identify referral patterns and may afford the district an opportunity to develop stronger prevention programs.

Finally, make certain fiscal monitoring; reporting of the System to Track Account for Children (STAC) process occurs monthly. In one district these reports were filed incorrectly. When an Administrative Intern discovered this error the forms were properly filed. The district ultimately received over $300,000 from the state as a direct result of filing these forms correctly.

19. Install photocopying monitoring devices on all copiers

When photocopying is not monitored by electronic devices abuse takes place. The cost to install monitoring devices is minimal and the results can be well worth the investment. One district saved $14,000 in paper and toner costs in the first year the monitoring devices were installed.

20. Replace desktop printers with networked high-volume multifunctional copiers

Replacing desktop printers can lower costs, save paper, and use less energy. Xerox officials confirm that operating costs are much lower when multifunctional copiers are used. Per copy savings whether black and white or colored are reported to be about 50%. One school in Wisconsin eliminated all inkjet and laser printers. All teachers and students now print to one of five multifunctional copiers. It is hoped that the acknowledged inconvenience of having to retrieve the documents will make students and teachers think more carefully about their decision to print.

21. Pull the plug on personal appliances

Many districts are banning the use of coffee pots, microwaves, radios, and other gadgets from the classrooms. This may seem a petty cost-cutting measure, but in reality, a large school system, such as Volusia County Fla. reportedly, can save as much as a half a million dollars annually on the utility bill. Removing small appliances from classrooms also can reduce insurance costs and improve safety by ensuring strict compliance with fire regulations.

22. Look closely at dependents claimed by employees receiving health insurance

The Palm Beach County, Fla. school system cut 1,500 people from its health insurance rolls after looking closely at dependents claimed by employees. Industry analysts say it's not unusual to find grown children, elderly relatives and neighbors listed as dependents. Cleaning the rolls saved the County $4 million annually – and those savings will be seen year after year.

23. Review district health insurance premium payment amount for retirees.

Districts that are paying health insurance premiums for retirees should regularly check for those employees who have become eligible for Medicare. Enrollment in the Medicare program may result in reduced regular health insurance premiums for the district. The district should not be redundantly paying primary insurance premiums for retirees who have primary coverage from Medicare.

24. Increase lawn mowing cycle

Most districts are on a preset lawn mowing cycle. Depending on the total acreage of the grass to be mowed increasing the lawn mowing cycle by only a day or two can decrease labor costs substantially.

25. Monitor overtime expenses

Uncontrolled overtime expense can substantially add to overall labor costs. Hourly employees working more than forty hours per week must be paid time and a half. In some circumstances employees regular salaries have been increased by 25 to 50% annually as a result of the lack of a regular system to monitor the overtime of employees. In some circumstances, for a brief period of time, it may be more economical to pay overtime to a current employee rather than hire an additional employee. Such arrangements however should be closely supervised.

26. Combine sports teams transportation

Sports teams' transportation can be a costly expense as these "runs" are all extra time earnings for bus drivers. Often two teams in different sports may be playing away games at two different schools but these schools are fairly close to each other. Using one bus rather than two, while slightly inconvenient, may result in budget savings.

CHAPTER FIVE

Intermediate Budget Reductions

The Immediate Budget Reductions are ones that a school board could authorize during the school year and reasonably expect to be in place no later than the beginning of the following school year.

1. Reduce the number of athletic teams and contests
2. Reduce coaching stipends based on decreased number of contests
3. Reduce Extra Curricular offerings and expenses
4. Influence reduction in BOCES Administrative Budget
5. Reduce BOCES Service requests
6. Study possibility of Shared Business Office
7. Study possibility of Shared Transportation and/or Maintenance Facility
8. Explore Shared Fuel Facility
9. Study possibility of Shared Food Service Director
10. Increase class size

11. Forego membership in State and National School Board Associations
12. Eliminate Kindergarten
13. Eliminate Drivers Education
14. Reduce or Eliminate Elementary Guidance Counselors
15. Eliminate Elementary Foreign Language
16. Reduce the number of Elementary School Librarians
17. Eliminate Gifted and Talented Programs
18. Eliminate use of Teacher Assistants
19. Eliminate Nurse Teacher positions
20. Reduce or eliminate Nursing services
21. Reduce Curriculum Development
22. Eliminate or reduce participation in out of district music, art and business competitions
23. Eliminate Marching Band
24. Reduce the number of Teacher Aide positions
25. Reduce the number of custodians/maintenance work
26. Reduce the number of food service workers
27. Reduce the number of teachers
28. Reduce the number of administrators
29. Study/reduce the number of Guidance Counselors at Middle and High Schools
30. Study the roles/responsibilities of Psychologists/ Social Workers and reduce as appropriate
31. Offer a meaningful retirement incentive that will entice senior employees to retire
32. Implement/Negotiate a four day work week during the summer.
33. Prepare a Contingency Budget
34. Consider privatizing custodial and/or transportation services
35. Introduce "pilot programs" rather than district wide implementation of new programs
36. Reduce Board of Education budget
37. Eliminate all "contingency" items in the budget.

38. Conduct bus routing study to modify routes as needed
39. Increase number of riders on each bus
40. Review bus stops and increase distances between stops
41. Discontinue bus transportation for students who live close to their school.
42. Stagger school start times
43. Drop "Block" scheduling
44. Review possible program duplication
45. Eliminate Intramural sports and after school activities
46. Identify "Sacred Cows" and consider eliminating them
47. Eliminate position of School Resource Officer
48. Eliminate Contract Substitutes
49. Reduce pay scale for Contract Substitutes
50. Deploy Administrators As Substitute Teachers

Here is a detailed explanation of what is involved in the Intermediate Budget Reductions with some specific examples of savings achieved by adopting these suggestions.

1. Reduce the number of athletic teams and contests

The New York State Public High School Athletic Association helped all districts in the State in the fall 2009 season. The Association approved a series of cost-cutting measures that it believed would maintain quality interscholastic athletics for the 585,000 student athletes in New York State who currently participate in high school athletics while reducing program costs.

a) Reduced the number of games teams can play during the regular season. For example in the basketball season instead of playing 24 games the Association approved a reduction in the game schedule to 20 games.

b) Limit how far teams can travel to play games. Member schools are limited in their out-of-state travel to competition with bordering states only. Among other things this would discontinue the increasingly common practice of having school baseball teams travel to the south at a huge expense to the district to play games in North and South Carolina and Florida.

c) Move or keep state championship games at a central location within the State.

d) Reduce the number of participants in state tournaments. This will reduce the number of classes and divisions in team and individual championship competition and reduce the participants in the championship games in individual and combination (team/individual) sports.

e) Limit the tournaments and scrimmages teams and individuals can participate in. For example, Varsity, Junior Varsity and Freshman teams are limited to two scrimmages and Modified teams are limited to one.

The question of the number of teams individual districts need requires a decision be made in response to the question, how many teams and in what sports are teams necessary and viable?

2. Reduce coaching stipends based on decreased number of contests

This proposed reduction will bring up the observation that most coaches currently work for a small stipend now. When these small stipends are broken into an hourly rate it becomes almost laughable. Regardless, coaches have annually been willing to work for this stipend. Is it reasonable to continue to pay a person the same amount of money for less work? Changes in these stipends will need to be re-negotiated prior to imposing them.

3. Reduce Extra Curricular offerings and expenses

The study of the number of extracurricular clubs and activities a district offers and their associated costs should be part of any budget reduction activity. One district with approximately 6000 students offered 209 clubs and activities to its middle and high school students. Stipends paid for each of these clubs and activities ranged from $600 to $1200. Some clubs had as few as three active members. In this particular district a 50% cut in clubs and activities was made. This resulted in a budget savings of $110,000.

In another district the teachers union actually proposed taking a 75% cut for the next two years in teacher stipends on the condition that at least some teaching assistant and teacher aide positions would be retained by using the money saved as a result of this cut. While this did not save the district any total dollars it did save some staff positions and demonstrated a valuable spirit of cooperation.

4. Influence reduction in BOCES Administrative Budget

BOCES Administrative Services are not optional payments by component districts although they should be monitored carefully by component district representatives. The BOCES organization is charged with the responsibility to make available to component districts a wide variety of services the district requests. Simply because the service is offered however does not mean that districts are required to or should necessarily request and ultimately purchase these services. BOCES Administrative costs are generally a function of the number and breadth of services offered by that BOCES.

5. Reduce BOCES Service requests

Generally BOCES Service requests costs increase every year. BOCES was created on the premise that by providing services in cooperation with other school districts the cost of the services would be less. Unfortunately in some cases the BOCES costs have risen so substantially for a variety of reasons that individual districts can offer these services more economically. Districts should review their BOCES Service Requests carefully each year and make appropriate adjustments. Even with BOCES Aid sometimes the required services can actually be provided at a lesser cost by a local district.

6. Study possibility of Shared Business Office

Several school districts have created a Shared Business Office with other districts in their region. Creation of these offices has resulted in cost savings. If this office is created through BOCES as a BOCES Service, this Service will probably be BOCES Aidable. Sharing positions such as Treasurers, Account Clerks, and Payroll Clerks is certainly worth considering. Sharing a Business Official can be more challenging however given the possibility of "divided loyalty."

7. Study possibility of Shared Transportation and/or Maintenance Facility

Some districts have created these facilities and have a record of continuing to provide safe transportation and efficient maintenance while saving taxpayers money.

8. Explore Shared Fuel Facility

Some districts have explored sharing fuel facilities with other districts and in some cases even with other branches of local government. There may even be grant money available to study this possibility.

9. Study possibility of Shared Food Service Director

The Food Service Director position is a critical one in any school district. The job responsibilities are very similar in each district which makes this an ideal position to consider sharing with another district or districts. This really amounts to increasing the span of control of one Director. Sharing this position through BOCES can even make the position BOCES Aidable which may be an additional method to save dollars while still maintaining a high level of service.

10. Increase class size

Class size and its effect on student achievement is an issue that has been researched for several years. The results of that research appear to be inconclusive. Much of the call for smaller class size is based on emotion and teacher union rhetoric not research. In a recent analysis of a few school districts, class size at the elementary level averaged 12.8 students. Other districts have elementary class sizes as high as 25. Averages are also computed in various ways. Some districts compute the average number of students in a grade level across the district, while others compute it by counting the number of students in a grade level in a school. Increasing class size at the elementary level, even by a few students, can lead to major cost savings.

In an analysis of school districts the Middle School class size averaged 15.5 students. Actual class size ranged from

11.8 to 22 students. At the high school level class size also averaged 15.5 students. Actual class size ranged from 12.4 to 20.4 students. Increasing class size at the middle and high school level can also lead to major cost savings.

11. Forego membership in State and National School Boards Associations

Board memberships in the State and National School Boards Associations, while allowable expenses, are not mandated under the law. Boards making the decision to forego association membership even for one year can set a tone for others in the district to follow. For example, in 2010 the annual membership dues of the New York State School Board Association for a school district with a $5 million budget were $3,250. For districts with a $24 million budget the dues are $7,865, for a $50 million budget the dues were $9,635. The maximum membership dues for a large district are $12,505.

12. Eliminate Kindergarten

Kindergarten is not a mandated program under State Education Law in many states. While there has been a movement in recent years to provide a Pre-K program, which the State has even funded in some cases, neither of these are mandated programs. If other program cuts are under consideration it is difficult not to give this idea some consideration.

13. Eliminate Drivers Education

Drivers Education is not a mandated program. It may be considered a "safety" issue in some communities but schools are not required to provide this instruction within their regular budget.

14. Reduce or Eliminate Elementary Guidance Counselors

Elementary Guidance Counselors are not required positions in a school district. Often these positions have been added to help manage the myriad of issues younger children are bringing to school. While this may be desirable, hard questions should be asked about the number and absolute necessity of these positions given the financial difficulties districts are facing.

15. Eliminate Elementary Foreign Language

Although the early grades may be the best time to teach students a foreign language, many schools are cutting the elementary programs. Foreign Language offerings in Elementary grades are not mandated programs. A survey from the Center for Applied Linguistics found that U.S. elementary schools have cut back on foreign language instruction during the last decade. About 25 percent of schools offered foreign language in 1997 but only 15 percent did so in 2007. In Pennsylvania, a Pittsburgh school eliminated some classes and Hempfield Area School District recently ended a 12-year old language program consisting of French and Spanish courses. The teachers of these programs lost their jobs. While there may be reasons in some communities to offer these opportunities these reasons should be reviewed in these challenging times, particularly if more "core" programs are under consideration for reduction.

16. Reduce the number of Elementary School Librarians

New York State mandates require only that students in 7th through 12th grade have school librarians. There is no requirement to have an Elementary School Librarian in each elementary school. Some districts choose to rotate librarians through their elementary schools which means librarians are working at several schools during the year. Librarians are certified teachers so the cost to staff each library with a certi-fied Library Media Specialist can be costly.

17. Eliminate Gifted & Talented Programs

These programs can be very beneficial to generally a small group of students. The programs are not mandated however. Care should be taken in decision making that programs which benefit many students academically are not reduced to provide special programming to a few students.

18. Eliminate use of Teacher Assistants

Teacher Assistants are certified to teach students under the general supervision of a certified teacher. Teacher Assistants often receive salaries that equal about one half of a certified teachers' salary. Teacher Aides on the other hand are not certified to teach under any circumstances. They are employed to assist in non-instructional duties. Teacher Aides salaries are much less, perhaps one quarter of a teachers' salary. Districts who employ Teacher Assistants should review their responsibilities and actual utilization, to be certain that they are required for the functions they are performing. Often Teacher Aides can perform the required functions at less expense.

19. Eliminate Nurse Teacher positions

Some districts employ Nurse Teachers who actually provide nursing services rather that provide student instruc-tion. Certified Nurse Teachers are part of the Teachers

Bargaining Unit and as such command a much higher salary than regular nurses. If the Nurse Teacher does not actually give instruction full time, there is no need to employ full time Nurse Teachers to provide nursing services.

20. Reduce or eliminate Nursing Services

While districts are required to provide students with school health services there is no requirement to have a full time nurse in each building. Districts can share the employment of health professionals or BOCES can provide the service.

21. Reduce Curriculum Development

Curriculum Development has been a necessary and worthwhile activity in most districts over the last few years. Boards should determine if the Curriculum Development that has been done has been implemented in the classrooms or if more implementation time is necessary. If more implementation time is needed the future development of curriculum could be delayed.

22. Eliminate or reduce participation in out of district music, art and business competitions

Most districts participate in the State Music Association solo competitions that lead to student participation in regional, statewide and even national ensembles. Many districts also fund the attendance at adjudication opportunities for ensembles and large groups. Art, business and vocational education students also have competitive opportunities at the State and National level. Some of these activities could be curtailed during challenging financial times.

23. Eliminate Marching Band

Many school districts pride themselves in their marching band. There is a certain amount of pride that comes with watching your school marching band come marching down the street leading your local parade. The costs associated with fielding a marching band however can be substantial. In addition to the teacher costs, there are uniforms and equipment upkeep and replacement costs, transportation costs as well as chaperone expenses.

Reduce Support Staff

Reducing Support Staff is one of the most difficult decisions that a school board makes. In some cases staff members have worked for the district for several years and have given excellent service. Additionally most support staff are residents of the district and vote there. The least traumatic reductions in staff can be made when a vacancy occurs either through resignation or retirement. Unfortunately the mind set in many districts is if someone has been in a position in the past the vacant position needs to be filled. This is not always the case and in these difficult financial times it is especially not the case. In the Appendix we have provided a sample Open Position Analysis Form which can be helpful in determining whether an open position needs to be filled. Between 75% and 85% of most school budgets consist of salary and benefits. The savings when a position is not filled can be substantial and is the most dramatic method to reduce expenses.

24. Reduce the number of Teacher Aide positions

In some districts Teacher Aide positions have been created to have an additional set of hands to perform clerical work, rather than have the Aide work directly with students. These positions and the responsibilities associated with them should be studied periodically to assure their necessity. In some cases various clerks and secretaries can add Aide responsibilities to their work load.

25. Reduce the number of custodians/maintenance workers

Studying the square footage of a building a custodian is responsible for is an excellent way to determine the appropriate number of custodians. Often there are huge differentials in the amount of square footage for which various custodians are responsible. The position of maintenance workers should also be examined periodically. A study of how Maintenance Work Orders are processed and handled by these workers is critical. Sometimes there are more efficient ways to handle these work orders which may result in more work being done by fewer numbers of workers.

26. Reduce the number of food service workers

Food service costs are primarily driven by the number of personnel involved in preparing and serving the food. Regular studies should be conducted of the work load and efficiency of the food service workers.

Reduce Professional Staff

Reducing Professional Staff is probably the most difficult reduction that is made in a school budget. Vacated positions determined to be appropriate for elimination is the easiest way to deal with these reductions. Every teacher position eliminated generates at least $55,000 in savings when salary and benefits are considered. No other reduction or elimination can generate savings close to this magnitude.

Changes in staffing levels are painful not just for the affected individuals and their families; they may also be detrimental to a district's culture and the community at large. Expect a strong, negative response from everyone concerned. Such a response should not however deter a board of education from making these difficult decisions when necessary for the overall good of the children, parents and taxpayers the district serves.

27. Reduce the number of teachers

This is a natural place to turn when looking to save money because salaries and benefits typically account for about three-quarters of a district's budget. A thorough staffing audit, independent class size research and a non-emotional consideration of teacher staffing needs will help to make these difficult decisions.

28. Reduce the number of administrators

Generally when people think about reducing professional staff the first thought is to reduce the number of administrators. Obviously the number of administrators a district has should be reviewed. It is worth noting that the span of control (the number of employees an administrator is responsible for) in schools is much greater than in industry and many other human services organizations. It is not unusual for a single principal to be responsible for the evaluation and supervision of between 20 and 100 or more staff members. This compares to responsibility for 6 - 20 employees in other settings. In addition a principal may be responsible for between 125 - 425 students.

Education Law requires every school district to have a Superintendent of Schools. This can be a shared position with another district. Education Law also requires that every school building must have a Principal. This position cannot be shared with another building unless a waiver is approved by the State Education Commissioner. Ironically the Commissioner will not approve a waiver as a cost saving measure. The Principal position can be filled by an administrator with other responsibilities as long as the administrator is designated as the full time Principal of a building. A superintendent of schools may serve simultaneously as a building principal only with the approval of the Commissioner of Education. School Districts are not required to have assistant principals in school buildings.

29. Study/reduce the number of Guidance Counselors at Middle and High School

As indicated previously often Guidance Counselor positions have been added to help deal with the increasingly severe problems students bring with them to school. The U.S. Department of Education's National Center for Education Statistics shows the current U.S. student-to-counselor ratio is 476:1. Most Guidance Counselors, other than the Counselor for graduating Seniors, will report that a small minority of students take up most of their time.

One suburban school district having a combined Middle School/High School population of less than 2000 students reported having 3 Middle School and 10 High School Counselors. This is a ratio of 154 students per counselor compared to the current U.S. student-to-counselor ratio of 476:1 students per counselor. This situation probably evolved over time because in easier financial times attention to such matters is not a priority.

30. Study the roles/responsibilities of Psychologists/ Social Workers and reduce as appropriate.

The specific roles of Psychologists and Social Workers need to be studied to avoid duplication of service, particularly in light of the number of Guidance Counselors employed in many districts. There is certainly a place for Psychologists (student testers) and Social Workers (individual and family problem solvers) but without regular study of these roles duplication and unaffordable services can creep in. Specific usage guidelines actually can be developed that demonstrate good stewardship of taxpayer dollars.

31. Offer a meaningful retirement incentive that will entice senior employees to retire.

Meaningful retirement incentives can be another way to reduce costs. Naturally such plans have pros and cons. Foremost among the disadvantages is the loss of experienced staff that may be your most valuable contributors to district culture and the quality of academic programs. On the other hand a district may benefit from the infusion of new ideas, attitudes and enthusiasm. Acceptance of an early retirement incentive by senior teachers or staff will have a significant financial impact on total salary expenditures if these positions are not filled. If the vacated positions need to be filled, less experienced teachers or staff can be hired at substantially lower salaries. Savings in salaries will also reduce the districts' portion of Social Security expense and possibly lower health insurance and pension costs.

One district had previously offered a retirement incentive of $20,000 to any teacher who would retire. No teacher opted for the incentive. The next year the district determined that under the established retirement criteria twenty teachers would be eligible. The Board increased the retirement incentive to $36,500 but stipulated that at least eight teachers must indicate they were willing to accept the incentive. Twelve teachers accepted the incentive. The district determined that of the twelve there was a need to replace four of the retirees. As a result the district did not replace eight retiring teachers. The total savings to the district was $856,686

32. Implement/Negotiate a four day work week during the summer.

One district experimented with this concept last summer through a special agreement with their support staff bargaining units. Basically they increased the number of hours worked during the four days to equal the number of days usually worked over five days. Overall the results were positive. Two observations were noted that were of some concern. Some employees needed to be reminded with some regularity of the need to work the additional time on the four work days. Some maintenance and custodial staff found the days very long especially if they were involved in very strenuous activity. Savings were achieved through decreased utility bills and employees who normally work year round appreciated the opportunity to work less days during the summer.

(A 4-Day Workweek "Pilot" Proposal is included in the Appendix.)

33. Prepare a Contingency Budget

District leaders who anticipate rejection of the proposed budget by district voters would be well serviced to prepare a Contingency Budget. A Contingency Budget is generally prepared and adopted by the school board when the voters reject the board's proposed budget. The Board can give voters one opportunity to re-vote on the initial proposed budget or a modified budget but after two rejected votes the board must adopt a contingency budget. The contingency budget may not result in a percentage increase in total spending over the district's total spending under the district budget for the prior year that exceeds the lesser of (1) the result obtained when computing 120 percent of the Consumer Price Index, or (2) 4 percent over the prior year's budget. The federal Bureau of Labor Statistics announced the Consumer Price Index for 2008. As a result of this announcement the contingency budget cap for the 2009-2010 school year is 4% which is lower than 120 percent of the Consumer Price Index.

Development of a Contingency Budget should be done with guidance from the district's financial advisor as it can be fairly complicated. Examples of expenditures that may **not** be included in a Contingency Budget would be:

1) New equipment
2) Public use of school buildings and grounds, except where there is no cost to the district but a district may charge a fee that meets or exceeds its actual costs.
3) Nonessential maintenance
4) Capital expenditures, except in emergency situations
5) Consultant services to review district operations and make necessary recommendations necessary for the creation of the budget.
6) Under some circumstances salary increases for non-instructional employees who are not members of a collective bargaining unit and employees designated by the Public Employment Relations Board as "management or confidential."

34. Consider privatizing custodial and/or transportation services

If this possibility has not been studied it should be. Savings may be possible. Legal advice should be sought as there may be prohibitions to changing existing arrangements. If the existing employees are offered positions by the private contractor this becomes much less of a concern. Also, generally the employees that fill these positions are district residents and voters. Unless this change is made carefully it may have a negative effect on the passage of the school budget.

35. Introduce "pilot programs" rather than district wide implementation of new programs.

There are good reasons beyond financial ones to implement new programs as "pilot programs" rather than district wide. These would include the concerns of large staff development activities and assessment opportunities. The financial savings would be substantial.

36. Reduce Board of Education budget

In addition to setting an example for other reductions it is possible that some board members are not as concerned about their expenses as they should be. Reductions could include such changes as limiting the number of board members who attend conferences, as well as considering the necessity of attending State and National Conferences each year.

37. Eliminate all "contingency" items in the budget.

The public generally refers to "contingency" items as "fluff." While it is impossible to budget for every item that may occur during the school year having a "cushion" in multiple categories of the budget is disingenuous. Zero-based budgeting procedures can really help with this concern.

38. Conduct bus routing study to modify routes as needed

Bus routes should be studied and reviewed annually. Changes in the age of students, proximity to the schools and parents desire to drive their children can all be contributing factors to changes in bus routes. In one district the bus driver reported that in one housing development no children rode his bus any day. A letter was sent to all the parents of the children in the development noting this observation and suggesting that as a cost savings measure the route would be discontinued on a certain date unless parents had an objection. No one objected and the route was discontinued.

39. Increase number of riders on each bus

Very few buses ever run to capacity, in most cases 55 students. Regular monitoring of the number of riders may point to the possibility of combining routes even though the ride may be a little longer for the riders involved.

40. Review bus stops and increase distances between stops.

Most states have regulations regarding the legal maximum distance between student pick up points. The distance may be different for elementary, middle and high school students. For example the difference between stops for elementary students may be 1 ½ miles whereas the distance for middle and high school stops might be 2 miles. Most school districts do not adhere to these regulations as a result of parental pressure. While some modification of these regulations may be appropriate some school districts have gone as far as offering door to door pick-up. This seems very extreme and obviously is not cost effective.

If a district chooses to modify the pick-up points the board should expect parents to counter these changes with their own creative solutions. In one rural district in the Southern Tier of New York State a parent actually moved his driveway to the opposite end of his property in order to increase the distance between stops and force the district to continue to pick his children up at his home rather than have the children walk to a neighbor's property.

41. Discontinue bus transportation for students who live close to their school.

Most states have suggested or mandated regulations regarding the transportation of students who live certain distances from their school. In New York State the regulation states that if an elementary student lives 1.5 miles or more from the school that student must be picked up by a school bus. The City of Rochester School District determined that if they discontinued bus transportation for students who live less than 1.5 miles from the school the district could save $1.2 million per year. Suburban districts around Rochester have varying policies regarding the distance from the elementary school students must live before transportation is provided. The Gates Chili Central School District provides transportation for all students with the exception of a small number who walk from their homes located near their school buildings. The West Irondequoit Central School District transports only elementary students who live more than 1.5 miles from their school. Other districts transport students who live 0.25 miles, 0.3, or 1 mile from their elementary school.

Many parents will object to any reduction in the distance districts use to determine when transportation will be provided. On the other hand, the Center for Disease Control and Prevention maintain more children should be encouraged to walk in an effort to increase physical activity and reduce child obesity.

42. Stagger school start times

Schools need to review the start times of their various buildings. There is plenty of research that supports the notion that elementary students perform better academically in the early morning than high school students. Districts should study their current busing schedule and school start times to see if starting schools at significantly different times would allow them to utilize their bus fleet and their drivers more economically. In Florida's St. Lucie County Schools start times were adjusted resulting in a saving of over $2 million. The district was able to reduce the number of buses used and have the buses used make more runs.

43. Drop "Block" scheduling

Block scheduling for students has been adopted in many school districts. While there are significant benefits for students and teachers there are also increased costs involved. California's Hayward Unified School District decided to end block scheduling at its' three high schools. Under the block scheduling plan students took four 90-minute classes per semester, equaling eight courses per year. The schools have adopted a more traditional schedule of six courses per year. The reduction in teaching staff resulted in a savings of about $1 million

44. Review possible program duplication

District academic programs need to be reviewed periodically to make certain there is no program or objectives duplication. In one district two special programs were developed and introduced in the 7-12 English Department. The programs sought to enhance reading, writing and collaborative skills in middle and high school students. As finances grew tighter the district reviewed the objectives of the special programs only to find that the same objectives were being covered as part of its regular English Language Arts curriculum. The special programs were discontinued. The savings to the district were nearly $260,000.

45. Eliminate Intramural sports and after school activities.

This suggestion is contrary to the desire of most parents. They would prefer the schools keep their children during the day as long as possible for personal, financial or scheduling reasons. Intramural sports and other after school activities are not required and the expense of providing advisors or supervisors can be costly.

46. Identify "Sacred Cows" and consider eliminating them.

Sacred cows vary from district to district but most school districts have them. In one district the sacred cow was "6th Grade Camp." In this district students from all elementary schools currently in 5th grade were invited to attend this camp in June. The idea was that the students would have the opportunity to get acquainted with everyone else who would be going into 6th grade (Junior High) in the Fall. By discontinuing this camp the district saved $51,000.

In another district the "Sacred Cow" was "neighborhood schools." In a survey done in the district "Retaining Neighborhood Schools" was the first priority of respondents to a question regarding what the district should preserve. When asked to define "neighborhood schools," people responded, "Giving students living in the neighborhood the opportunity to attend that school." After a thorough analysis the district found that in many cases parents chose to send their children to a different school based on perceptions or beliefs that the school they chose for their children was "better." It turned out that "Neighborhood Schools" really meant a school in a residential neighborhood. Once residents realized the true definition the district was able to move forward with consolidating the neighborhood schools which resulted in cost savings of over $300,000 for district taxpayers.

47. Eliminate position of School Resource Officer

Several years ago the Federal Government offered a three year grant program (no cost to the local district) to place police officers in schools. Hundreds of school districts accepted the "free money." As always happens with this type of grant eventually the Federal money ran out or was substantially reduced and districts were faced with the difficult decision of continuing the program at district expense solely or discontinuing the program. In this case parents, teachers, administrators and some students indicated they felt safer with the police officers physically present in their school and wanted the program to continue. As a result the cost became a total district responsibility.

Administratively several issues surfaced as part of this program. Would there be a "substitute" police officer provided when the regular School Resource Officer took vacation, was sick or needed personal time? Who would conduct the supervision and evaluation of the officer, a school administrator, who actually knew what the officer was doing, or his supervising officer located at the police station? Who would reconcile the differences in the rights and responsibilities of the school administrator in dealing with students versus the rights and responsibilities of a police officer dealing with students? Even if these differences could be acceptably resolved there remained the issue of who will be responsible for the salary and benefits of the officer? Districts should also examine whether the peer mentoring and anti-bullying programs that have been instituted more recently cover at least a portion of the responsibilities generally assumed by a School Resource Officer.

48. Eliminate Contract Substitutes

In order to provide continuity and to save calling substitute teacher's everyday some districts have chosen to hire Contract Substitutes. These substitute teachers report to a particular school every day throughout the school year. If they are not required to fill in for an absent teacher they do office work or have other responsibilities. While there is certainly a measure of convenience to have this position it is a costly convenience. A Contract Substitute is on a contract salary which may be more than twice the cost of a daily substitute.

49. Reduce pay scale for Contract Substitutes

Contract Substitutes as discussed in the previous item can be a costly convenience. If the district feels strongly that Contract Substitutes are necessary perhaps the pay scale could be reduced, given the fact that work is hard to find in many communities as a result of today's economy.

50. Deploy Administrators As Substitute Teachers

The Broward County School District in Florida has asked all district administrators to help save the district money by agreeing to go into classrooms to substitute teach. All administrators who are certified to teach will replace other substitute teachers twice a month. The district is projecting an annual saving of $200,000.

CHAPTER SIX

Long Term Budget Reductions

This final group of possible budget reductions is entitled Long Term Budget Reductions. As the name implies these reductions are ones that a board could have as long term goals to be accomplished over the next one to three years.

1. Study merger/consolidation with a neighboring district
2. Send high school students to a neighboring district on a tuition basis.
3. Negotiate "no increase" employment contracts
4. Negotiate the elimination of "step" increases in contracts
5. Negotiate the elimination of "longevity" increases in contracts
6. Negotiate the discontinuation of the practice of paying additional salary for completing a Masters Degree and graduate courses

7. Limit tuition reimbursement to the equivalent tuition of a state school regardless of where the course is completed
8. Negotiate a lower premium health care program
9. Negotiate an increase in the contribution employees make toward their health insurance premiums
10. Negotiate a lower district health insurance premium contribution for all new employees
11. Investigate the use of windmills
12. Ask bargaining units to forego previously negotiated increases
13. Negotiate a one week "skip" of salary for all district employees.
14. Ask employees bargaining units to accept a salary reduction.
15. Negotiate a limited amount of unpaid vacation time.
16. Investigate K – 11 option
17. Investigate a 4 day week for instruction
18. Urge passage of several proposed mandate relief measures
19. Offer State retirement incentives and institute a "no unnecessary replacement" policy
20. Change Paid Leave provisions
21. Share a Superintendent of Schools

Here is a detailed explanation of what is involved in the Long Term Budget Reductions with some specific examples of savings achieved by adopting these suggestions.

1. Study merger/consolidation with a neighboring district

The concept of merging two or more districts has been around for many years. A few districts have successfully merged. The results have been greater opportunities for students and significant cost savings for taxpayers.

A merger requires voter approval in both districts proposing the merger. In the past securing this voter approval as been extremely difficult. It remains to be seen whether the significant financial challenges we currently face will cause more voters to support a proposal for merger of their school district.

In Pennsylvania Governor Edward G. Rendell entered his state into the debate about consolidation of school districts as part of his budget address to the legislature in February 2009. The governor recommended the wholesale consolidation in the number of school districts from 501 to 100. His recommendation included the establishment of a commission to hold public hearings and within one year approve no more than two plans for reorganization. The General Assembly would have the opportunity to vote on the two plans. If they chose not to act the State Board of Education would hold another set of public hearings followed by a binding decision on one of the plans. As of this writing his recommendations continue to languish in the abyss of non-support.

In New York State a state commission headed by Thomas R. Suozzi, the Nassau County executive, issued a report in December 2008 that called for consolidating school districts with fewer than 1,000 students " … as a remedy for easing the crushing school property tax burden our state faces." No action has been taken on the commission's recommendations.

A survey released in January 2009 by the Indiana University's Center for Evaluation and Education Policy found that 66 percent of respondents said they would oppose combining their school district with another one. This high percentage of opposition despite the fact that 50 percent agreed that combining districts would expand learning opportunities for students; 49 percent said it would save tax dollars; and 45 percent agreed it would enhance student achievement.

Obviously this is not an easy recommendation to pursue but one that may well become necessary even by legislation in the future.

2. Send high school students to a neighboring district on a tuition basis.

This decision may be nearly as controversial as merging with another district but it does have the potential for significant financial savings while preserving the local elementary school. One plan might be to maintain the elementary school for students K – 8 and pay tuition for high school students to attend other neighboring high schools. The Wyoming Central School District in New York State has done this quite successfully since 1991.

3. Negotiate "no increase" employment contracts.

If a school district has contracts in place this will be very difficult to attain as unions will typically want to maintain the salary and benefits they have previously negotiated for their members. If a district is at the beginning of contract negotiations this becomes more realistic however. Negotiators do have to be careful not to give the union grounds for claiming they are not negotiating in good faith.

Past experience demonstrates that school boards often complain to the public that there is nothing they can do about salary and benefit increases because they have been previously negotiated with employee unions. This claim is somewhat disingenuous. The fact is that all employee contracts require approval by the Board of Education. So, at some point the Board approved the very contracts that they now claim they can do nothing about. Board members need to remember this fact and lay out realistic guidelines for their negotiation team as they begin negotiations. In these economic times, with the possibility of continuing decreases in State Aid and more local taxpayer concern about their ability to pay their property taxes, school boards do need to be very careful. Negotiating contracts that continue union member employment but with no increase in salary and perhaps even a greater employee contribution toward the increasing cost of health insurance is not an unreasonable goal.

Many employers in the private sector have told employees there will be no increase in their salary, some for more than one year. Some employers are even being forced to decrease salaries. Unfortunately, for some reason, school board members are generally not willing to take this strong position when it comes to bargaining units associated with education. With personnel costs accounting for 75% - 85% of the total school budget such a negotiation stance may be necessary at this time.

4. Negotiate the elimination of "step" increases in contracts.

"Step" increases are basically automatic annual salary increases that are neither earned under any specific criteria or even necessarily appropriate for everyone in a bargaining unit. Such "steps" often incur a 2.5% to 3% salary increase. Most teacher bargaining units give these automatic increases no thought when they present their initial salary proposal to a district. In other words salary proposals are for "new" money, not "step" increases.

5. Negotiate the elimination of "longevity" increases in contracts.

Similar to "step" increases longevity increases are basically increases given for completing another year of work. There is no criteria for earning this increase such as competency, improvement in anything, student performance or otherwise, just because another year of work has been completed.

6. Negotiate the discontinuation of the practice of paying additional salary for completing a Masters Degree and graduate courses.

Taxpayers are spending billions of dollars each year rewarding teachers for earning a Master's Degree, which in most states is a requirement of continuing in their teaching position. Not only do teachers earn increased money for the Master's and the graduate hours it takes to complete the degree but this increase is added to their salary calculation throughout their career. Another indication that this practice should be discontinued is the fact that many new teachers are coming to their first teaching position already with a Masters Degree that they have paid for themselves. In Chicago Illinois 43 percent of recent hires had a Masters Degree.

Payment for graduate hours beyond the Master's should certainly be limited. Payment for graduate courses that directly correlate to the area the teacher is teaching, future career aspirations or earning advanced certification through the National Board for Professional Teaching Standards might be appropriate. Taking graduate courses simply to boost a teacher's salary is a practice that needs to be discontinued.

7. Limit tuition reimbursement to the equivalent tuition of a state school tuition regardless of where the course is completed.

If districts reimburse teachers for completing graduate courses reimbursement should be limited to the tuition rate charged at state schools. This proposal does not restrict teachers from taking graduate courses at an institution of their choice, public or private; it simply ties the reimbursement rate to the State school rate.

One district that studied this option determined that 84% of its' teachers chose to attend private schools. The total amount reimbursed was $1.2 million. If the reimbursement rate had been tied to the State school tuition rate the savings would have been $680,000.

8. Negotiate a lower premium health care program.

All districts need to "shop" for lower premium health care programs on an annual basis. Some programs offer the same benefits or benefits that are very similar to the existing program but at significantly reduced rates, sometimes with savings of $1 million or more. Most unions are willing to consider a different health care program as long as they can be assured of little or no change in benefits to their members.

The West Seneca Central School District in Western New York has controlled its health insurance costs considerably by paying its districts' union an annually negotiated fixed fee and having the union handle the health insurance program entirely.

9. Negotiate an increase in the contribution employees make toward their health insurance premiums.

It is not unusual for health insurance premiums to increase by 10% or more each year. One study found the majority of teachers contribute 15% of the total cost. Unless this contribution rate is increased the district assumes more and more of the cost each year.

10. Negotiate a lower district health insurance premium contribution for all new employees.

During negotiations most unions are very reluctant to agree to increase the contribution their current members make toward the total cost of health insurance premiums. Most unions are more willing to agree with the district setting a higher contribution rate for new employees. These new employees are not union members as yet and therefore they have made no investment in the union.

11. Investigate the use of windmills.

Some districts that have conducted a study to determine the feasibility of using windmills to generate power have found that savings are possible, even with the capital outlay up front. The Perkins High School in Ohio installed 60-foot turbines and are estimating a reduction in utility bills of 11% annually. Some grants may be available for such a study.

12. Ask bargaining units to forego previously negotiated increases.

Experience has shown that this request is generally not met with enthusiasm or agreement. In these extremely unusual times it may still be worth asking. Teachers in Denver, Colorado in the fall of 2009 overwhelmingly approved a revised contract which lowered a previously negotiated salary increase of 4.15% to a 2.5% cost-of-living raise and 1.65% stipend if the economy improves.

13. Negotiate a one week "skip" of salary for all district employees.

Surprisingly this is one cost reduction that has been suggested by some employees. It is viewed as a "fair and equitable" response to the financial issue and eliminates long term "pain." Once the week is passed, the savings have occurred without further tension.

14. Ask employee bargaining units to accept a salary reduction.

A skeptic might argue that such a request would never be received favorably by any employee bargaining unit. The facts show otherwise. In the Fall of 2009 Hawaii's public school teachers ratified a new two-year labor contract with the State. The Hawaii State Teachers Association 13,000 members voted to support the state Board of Education contract proposal which will result in salary cuts of almost 8 percent. The contract will require teachers on a 10-month schedule to take 17 unpaid days off each year. Teachers on year-round schedules will be furloughed 21 days a year. All furlough days fall on Friday. The down side is that to allow the furlough days to occur students will also have a furlough day each time. Obviously this will reduce the number of days of instruction students will receive.

15. Negotiate a limited amount of unpaid vacation time.

Employees in one district agreed to a limited amount of unpaid vacation time during the current year. Ten month employees agreed to pare their vacations by up to three days. Twelve month employees agreed to scale up their working days by two-and-a-half days. The district estimates savings of approximately $200,000 through these changes.

16. Investigate K – 11 option

Many students are ready for college after completing 11th grade. Some would even suggest that 12th grade is a waste of time for these students. They would be better served by having the opportunity to advance to a college environment. This option would require State Legislature approval. Other countries around the world including Canada currently have this model in place. It has been a successful model for their students and is worth investigating. The potential cost savings are enormous.

17. Investigate a 4 day week for instruction

It appears that many school districts are already researching this option as a cost saving measure. Primary savings would be in the areas of utility and transportation costs. This option would also require legislative approval but the State Education Department might be persuaded to allow a district to "experiment" with this idea if it was thoroughly developed and supported by a local community.

Advantages mentioned for studying this idea could be possible improvements in student attendance and discipline – presumably because students could be more effectively engaged in learning if they attended for longer periods on fewer days.

Reservations regarding this idea might include the impact on families, having to make alternative child care arrangements for young children, and perhaps leaving middle and high school youth unattended. A second reservation could be the impact on learning. Could younger children handle the longer school day that would be required to compensate for the fewer number of days?

Finally, the U.S. education system is frequently criticized for providing less instructional time than is common in other industrialized nations. In some past years, adding instructional time has been a leading collective bargaining goal for school districts. Furthermore, this year national leaders have indicated they are in favor of increasing instructional time by extending the school year.

In September 2009 the Niagara Catholic School in Niagara Falls, NY launched an experiment with a four-day week. The school will be closed each Monday. Officials estimate they will save $10,000 in operating costs while faculty and staff will continue at the same pay and benefits level as before. As a non-public school, Niagara Catholic is not bound by state requirements for offering 180 days of instruction.

18. **Urge immediate passage of several proposed mandate relief measures that have been under consideration for some time.** *(Examples given are from New York State)*

a) **Exempting school districts from the Wicks Law.** School districts will be exempted from Wicks Law's requirements for the next five years. The Wicks Law requires school districts to have separate construction contracts with each construction specialty group, i.e. Electrical, Plumbing and Heating, etc. rather than one General Construction contract.

(While this measure will help school districts when they are entering into construction contracts it will have no immediate impact or benefit to a districts operating budget.)

b) **Allowing districts to access certain reserve funds.** This proposal would allow districts to withdraw limited amounts of excess funds in an employee benefits accrued liability reserve fund with the approval of the State Comptroller to maintain educational programs.

(This measure helps only districts that have excess funds in its employee benefits accrued liability reserve fund.)

c) **Reforming pensions.** The proposal would remove pension enhancements added after the creation of the Tier IV retirement category, which will allow districts to reduce growth in their pension costs, one of the fastest-growing local government cost drivers.

(This may reduce growth in the future but will do nothing this current year as the district contribution rates have already been established.)

d) **Reforming procurement.** This would allow school districts additional contracting flexibility by increasing existing bidding thresholds and allowing them to piggyback onto existing contracts.

e) **Reducing paperwork.** This proposal would streamline existing reporting requirements and eliminate required reports that are outdated or no longer serve a public policy purpose.

(Until specific reports to be eliminated are identified this reform has no value.)

f) Delay the effective date of mandates. Any new mandate with a cost would not be implemented sooner than the following school year to allow districts the opportunity to build their costs into their budget.

(No saving impact this current school year. Simply delays potential increased costs for one year.)

19. Offer State retirement incentives and institute a "no unnecessary replacement" policy

Every year rumors abound that the State will provide districts with the opportunity to offer a retirement incentive to a group of qualified employees. Such State options can be very beneficial financially to districts but adopting them should be studied very carefully to make certain they have the desired outcome for the eligible employees and the district.

As noted earlier, districts also have the option of developing its' own retirement incentive although it must be negotiated with the appropriate union. When such an incentive is coupled with a "no unnecessary replacement" policy the cost savings can be significant.

20. Change Paid Leave provisions

Unused sick day and vacation day provisions should be reviewed regularly. There should be a cap on the amount of paid leave an employee can accumulate. Unused days should be subject to a "use them or lose them" provision. Without such a cap a district could find itself in a difficult financial situation if forced to make a large cash payment when a long time employee or group of employees retire with stockpiled paid leave. It is not unusual for long time employees to be owed tens of thousands of dollars. Such cases can cause great difficulty for a district that is forced to pay out this kind of money to a retiree while simultaneously cutting academic programs or raising taxes.

21. Share a Superintendent of Schools

In most states there is continuing pressure to reduce or eliminate levels of government to reduce the tax burden on homeowners and businesses. As a result many districts particularly in Iowa, Michigan, New Jersey and Virginia have studied the option of sharing a superintendent of schools. The location of the collaborating districts and the proximity of their various school buildings will impact the feasibility of such a plan.

Salary and benefits savings are not the only part of this concept's allure. With one chief executive, districts gain the benefit of combined purchasing power. One superintendent may have the ability to implement best practices and improve administrative efficiency in all involved districts. There may also be the opportunity for collaboration and cost-effective curriculum planning, testing, curriculum mapping, hiring practices, academic reporting, compliance, and internal operations controls.

Sharing a superintendent would also present some unique challenges. How will the boards of different districts interact? How will the superintendent's evaluation be handled? Would there be any long term impact on student achievement under a shared arrangement and if so, what would that impact be? Could the diverse culture, morays and folklore of different districts be adequately traversed by a shared superintendent?

CHAPTER SEVEN

Revenue Enhancers

A s opposed to budget reductions, the Revenue Enhancers listed below are possible ways that districts may be able to increase the revenues coming into the district's operating budget.

1. Reduce Fund Balance
2. Plan on proposing a major increase of the local property tax
3. Institute a "Use of Facilities" fee
4. Explore grant opportunities
5. Create a School Foundation
6. Restructure existing "Debt Service"
7. Explore the benefits of an Energy Performance Contract

1. Reduce Fund Balance

Governor Paterson of New York State has indicated that school districts have reported they have over $1.3 billion of uncommitted reserves which have been building up over time. He has also proposed mandate relief measures which would allow school districts to more easily utilize theses funds to help balance their financial needs. Districts should be careful in this regard not to reduce their fund balances to an "unsafe" level. On the other hand the amounts the districts have reported in many cases do seem excessive. Some states limit the size of reserves to an unreasonably low percentage of the budget. New York State for example sets the limit at 5 percent. The Government Finance Officers Association recommends that government entities, such as school districts maintain an unrestricted fund balance no less than 5 to 15 percent of operating revenues or no less than one to two months of regular, general fund operating expenditures. Board members need to remember while these reserves are "rainy day funds" they are also local taxpayer funds and should be used when necessary to help prevent tax increases.

2. Plan on proposing a major increase of the local property tax

It is important to know the amount of expense increase that could lead to a percentage increase in the property tax rate, not the tax levy. For example in a smaller district if expenses are increased by $50,000 this would lead to a 1% increase in the tax rate. In a large district $225,000 increase in expenditure would lead to a 1% increase in the tax rate. If a Board determines that a certain level of increased expense is necessary and acceptable they should also know the impact of that increase on the tax rate.

3. Institute a "Use of Facilities" fee.

Generally school districts are reluctant to institute these fees because most community members feel the school is available for use without cost because it is a community facility, paid for by the community. In New York State when voters of the school district fail to pass the annual school budget, which puts the district into a contingency budget situation, the district must assess a "Use of Facilities" fee. Taxpayers might be open to this fee in other circumstances if it was explained that the fee will help hold down property tax increases.

In Beaufort County, South Carolina the County School Board instituted a fee for facility use. Any organization not affiliated with the district must pay these fees. For example, for four hours of use $100 is charged for most athletic fields and stadiums. For gyms, locker rooms, multi-purpose rooms, cafeterias and kitchens a $115 fee is assessed. The fee for use of theatres and performing arts centers is $590.

4. Explore grant opportunities.

Unfortunately this suggestion is one that is always put forth when people are suggesting ways to reduce expenses or pay for new programs. While there are grants still available their availability has been greatly reduced and those available are being sought by an increasing number of applicants. Grant writing is an art that many school administrators simply do not have. Grants generally have a long lead time from application to approval, to receiving the dollars. Grants are certainly worth exploring, however everyone should be realistic in their expectations and be aware of the time constraints. Grants are not a quick fix solution for filling funding gaps. They will also be available generally for only very specific purposes and time frames.

5. Create a School Foundation

Educational foundations have been used by private schools for years as a way to supplement tuition income. This is a potential revenue producer that should be explored by public school districts. A foundation is governed by a separate board with a mission statement, bylaws and procedures for raising and distributing the raised funds. The school attorney should be involved in setting up the foundation so an appropriate "arms length" relationship from the district itself is created. Even foundations with modest resources can provide supplies for special projects or teacher training opportunities. Those with more extensive resources may be able to provide computers and other technology to the district.

6. Restructure existing "Debt Service"

Debt service is generally defined as the long term money a school owes for construction, buses or other items that can be financed over a long term, usually ten to thirty years. Depending on the terms of the original financing it may be worth asking the District Financial Advisor to investigate the possibility of restructuring this debt. This is similar to refinancing the mortgage on a home. Obviously restructuring the debt over a longer period of time adds significantly to the total overall debt, which may not be a desirable outcome. Such a restructuring, particularly if a lower interest rate is obtained, may reduce costs on an annual basis.

7. Explore the benefits of an Energy Performance Contract

After the 1979 energy crisis, districts in the Northeast partnered with utility companies and energy specialist firms to analyze consumption patterns. Some entered into energy performance contracts, installing monitoring systems and efficient equipment to control heat, hot water and air conditioning units. These contracts saved substantial amounts of money. The short term value of these agreements is that the district has no capital expense. Costs for improvements, often spread over the contract's lifetime, are based on the difference between the old energy costs and the savings generated by the more efficient equipment. When the contract expires, the district keeps the equipment and all future savings. In some states an energy performance contract may be eligible for state aid reimbursement. Perhaps it is time to revisit the benefits of these programs.

CHAPTER EIGHT

Budget Development

How the local budget is developed has tremendous impli-cations on the final outcome of the budget and may even have an impact on its passage or rejection by district voters. Some districts have the Superintendent of Schools and his staff develop the budget which is then presented to the Board of Education for review and adoption. Some districts have the Board of Education directly involved in budget development through a Board committee. In other districts a community committee is charged with the task of developing the budget for presentation to the Board.

Regardless of the process utilized to develop the budget someone or some group of people need to decide what the priorities of the budget will be. In other words what will be funded? Some districts have found a Priority Based Budget Planning document to be useful. A copy of this document is included in the Appendix. The document could be given to various constituencies, Board of Education members, administrators, teachers and community members. Results would be tallied by group as well as overall responses. Such a process would provide a wealth of useful data.

Budget Development Methods

Not only is the process utilized to develop the budget important in terms of who decides but the actual method used to development the budget is also critically important. Below are six principle approaches to budgeting: incremental budgeting: line item budgeting: program budgeting: the planning, programming and budgeting system (PPBS): zero-based budgeting: and site-based budgeting. It would be useful for every district to review their current method to be certain it is the most effect for them or if an alternative approach might be more beneficial.

1) **Incremental budgeting** has traditionally been the most common budgetary technique used by school districts. In this system the previous year's budget is used as the baseline for the new budget. Adjustments are made through percentage increases applied to the budget as a whole. State legislators often use an incremental budgeting process because it is simple and easy to explain to the general public. The disadvantage of incremental budgeting is that the current conditions are considered only minimally and no evaluation of past performance is required.

2) **Line item budgeting** like incremental budgeting relies on previous budgets for starting point data. It differs from incremental budgeting in that each line in the budget receives individual consideration. Percentage increases or decreases may be applied to one or more lines of the budget. The objective of the expenditure becomes the focus of attention. The

disadvantage of this system is a strong tendency to perpetuate the status quo.

3) **Program budgeting** organizes the budget by the major functions of the district often using State required budget codes. The function may then be linked back to an individual who has organizational or fiscal responsibility. Though the superintendent and board remain in control of the final decisions regarding the budget, program budgeting provides for greater input from staff and the community than line item or incremental budgeting.

4) **Planning, Programming and Budgeting System (PPBS)** links the budgeting process to programs through planning evaluation processes integrated into the systems. The process is highly complex, requiring both sophisticated technology and highly trained individuals for successful implementation. Its impact may be seen in the current emphasis on establishing goals, measuring progress toward those goals, and using the information obtained in the development of future budgets.

5) **Zero-based budgeting** is based on the premise that each year's budget starts with zero and is built anew with justification for the inclusion of each item. The budget is developed through the use of decision packages that specify program goals and outcomes and the consequences of alternative funding levels. These decision packages are then ranked in order of importance. Generally speaking, there will be two groupings of decision packages 1) those that are mandated by statute required for basic operation and 2) discretionary packages. This author prefers the zero based

budgeting approach as it has been extremely helpful in controlling costs and limiting the status quo in budgeting.

6) **Site based budgeting** enables staff members in schools and school systems to engage in decision-making regarding the expenditure of funds. This process commonly begins with revenue projections and allocations to program areas and buildings by the superintendent and board. Each building decision-making committee develops goals and objectives for the building and a budget designed to meet those goals within the parameters provided by the administration and board. Site based budgeting has many advantages, including building staff's sense of responsibility for and control over their funds. There is a danger however; those building budget managers' varying levels of skill will result in inequities both in funding and in the wise use of funds.

CHAPTER NINE

Now What?

Ibelieve public education is at a significant crossroad. As I said earlier, I predict that beginning with the 2011-2012 school year, if not sooner, we will see record numbers of school budgets fail for lack of voters support UNLESS school board members and district administrators step up and make the difficult but necessary financial reductions. District voters generally don't want to vote their local school district budgets down but they will be left with no responsible choice.

Government entities at all levels, Federal, State, County and Local need to hear and respond to the plea of taxpayers. "Enough is Enough!" Such a plea does not mean taxpayers are not supportive of the government programs including the education of children in the public school. What it does mean is that despite their best intentions and desires, costs have simply gotten so out of hand that they do not have the money to support even the most important and critical programs anymore.

So what can individuals or groups of people do about the impending crisis in public education finance? The first step is to acknowledge that Federal Stimulus money has been used up, our states are nearly bankrupt and our local taxpayers are fed up with increasing taxes.

After this first step has been acknowledged specific actions for various groups might include the following:

Board of Education members and school administrators can accept their legal responsibility to control school spending. As this book points out there are many options that can be used to control school spending. The challenge is to choose some options even though few of them are easy.

Community members and taxpayers can engage members of their Board of Education members and school administrators in conversation about the reality of the financial situation and offer their preferences in terms of specific options for controlling school costs.

Teachers and other district employees can indicate their understanding of the reality of the financial situation by indicating their willingness to make some sacrifices given the fact that employee costs make up such a large portion of any school budget.

Students can participate in district wide conversations about controlling costs by suggesting areas where they would be willing to bear a share of the pain.

Together people can make a difference! Together people can work to make public education even better than it is today despite the financially challenging times we are facing. This can happen as a result of people's creativity, willingness to share, sacrifice and determination.

APPENDIX

1. Open Position Analysis Form

2. 4-Day Workweek "Pilot" proposal

3. Priority Based Budget Planning

4. What is The Teaching and Learning Institute?

Open Position Analysis Form

Position: _____

Building: _____

<u>Questions:</u>

1. Is this a State mandated position? Yes / No

2. What does the position entail?

   _____

   _____

   _____

3. How does that position impact students?

   _____

   _____

   _____

4. Are there other ways to deliver the services for the students?

   _____

   _____

   _____

5. Who else is impacted?
   - ❑
   - ❑

6. Can the position **<u>not</u>** be filled? (Circle one) **Not Fill / Need to Fill**
   - ❑ If <u>not</u> filled, what changes need to be made for the students?
   - ❑ If <u>not</u> filled, whom do we need to contact?

7. Why do you believe the position **should** or **should not** be filled?

_____

_____

_____

_____

Any other information relating to this recommendation:

_____

_____

I make the following recommendation:

Circle one: Do <u>not</u>
fill position /Fill position

_____   _____

Supervising Administrator   **Date**

I have reviewed the information
and the Supervising Administrators' recommendation.

<u>support</u> / <u>do not support</u>

_____   _____

Assistant Superintendent   **Date**

I have reviewed the information
and the Supervising Adminis
trators' and Assistant Superintendent's recommendation.

<u>support</u> / <u>do not support</u>

_____   _____

Superintendent of Schools   **Date**

Please put an "X" beside the action required,

Do **Not** Fill Position _____   Fill Position _____

4-Day Workweek "Pilot" Proposal

History:

In a time of economic struggle, school districts are looking for creative ways to continue to offer outstanding educational programs to students without placing the state and federal funding crisis (decreased school aid) on the backs of the local taxpayers. This current financial problem necessitates "out of the box" thinking that delivers affordable answers.

One of the "out of the box" ideas that seems to be on the educational horizon is the 4-day workweek scenario. It appears that many school districts are researching this concept and some have even attempted implementation. While the idea does have support on both sides of the issue, there does not seem to be a clear and definitive answer to how successful a 4-day week would actually be when applied to school districts in our county.

Understanding that in the future the concept of a 4-day school week may indeed require more significant attention, a 4-day workweek "pilot" does warrant consideration.

Proposal:

Beginning July 1, 2010 and extending through August 21, 2010, the _____ Central School District current 5-day workweek would change to a 4-day workweek schedule (Monday through Thursday). With this change, the 37.5 hours of work that are now spread over 5 days would be applied over 4 days. As a result, the 7.5 hours per day would change to 9.375-hours day.

5-day:	**4-day:**
Monday-Friday	Monday-Thursday
7.5 hours/day	9.375 hours/day

Though there are some advantages to making this kind of programmatic change, the greatest advantage would be the ability of the school district to "work" and "feel" the actual effects of a 4-day workweek on a limited scope. (This pilot would <u>not</u> directly affect students and 10-month employees.)

Possible Other Advantages:

- ❑ Longer days would allow for more combination of summer maintenance tasks.
- ❑ School buildings would be closed on the 5th day resulting in potential energy savings.
- ❑ 12-month staff would have the 5th day off each week during the pilot time.
- ❑ District would strongly encourage <u>all</u> employees to move to direct deposit for payroll purposes.
- ❑ Other…

Possible Disadvantages:

- ❑ Longer work days for 12-month employees
- ❑ Productivity could decrease due to longer work days
- ❑ Community would not have access to buildings on 5th day
- ❑ Community could view this as another day off for employees and not recognize the extension of the hours each day.
- ❑ Other…

Contractual Units Affected by Change:

- All 12-month employees
  - o Secretaries
  - o Administrative Council
  - o Unions
  - o District Office Employees
  - o Individual Contract Employees
- Any "11-month" employees
  - o School Counselors
  - o School Social Workers and Psychologists

Possible next steps...

1. Board of Education discussion
2. Board of Education approval to engage in discussion with affected bargaining units
3. Discussion with affected bargaining units
4. Board of Education Discussion and Approval of 4-day pilot
5. Memorandums of Agreement developed
6. Public communication of change
7. Implementation July 1, - August 21, 2010
8. Comprehensive internal review of pilot program no later than September 30, 2010 with report to the Board of Education at a subsequent meeting.

Priority Based Budget Planning
Developed by TLI Inc. 2009

Definitions

Level 1: Programs and services **VITAL** for our school district

Level 2: Programs and services **NECESSARY** for our school district

Level 3: Programs and services **DESIRABLE** for our school district

Level 4: Programs and services **OPTIONAL** for our school district

Instructions: Please rank each item below as Level 1, 2, 3 or 4.

TOPIC/AREA	RANKING
Administrator Supplies	
Adult Education	
Art Supplies	
Athletic Teams	
Basic Building Maintenance	
Board Development	
BOCES Services	
Business Instruction	
Classroom Equipment	

TOPIC/AREA	RANKING
Co-curricular Activities	
Communications/Newsletter etc	
Conference Attendance (faculty)	
Conference Attendance (BOE)	
Driver Education	
Elementary Guidance	
Elementary School Librarians	
Field Trips	
Financial Planning Services	
Foreign Language Elementary	
Foreign Language Middle School	
Gifted and Talented Program	
Maintain current number of Teachers	
Maintain current number of Custodians, Cleaners, Clerks	

TOPIC/AREA	**RANKING**
Maintain current number of Administrators	
Maintain current number of Teaching Assistants	
Maintain current number of Teacher Aides	
Maintain current busing policies	
Membership in NYSSBA/NASB	
Musical Equipment	
Nursing Services	
Professional Journals	
Pre-Kindergarten	
Retain Elementary class size	
Retain Secondary class size	
Retain current level of Special Education programs	
Retain current Unappropriated Fund Balance	

TOPIC/AREA	RANKING
Staff Development	
Summer School-Elementary	
Summer School-Secondary	
Teacher Supplies	
Technology	
Textbooks Elementary	
Textbooks-Secondary	

Comments: _____

_____

_____

_____

Form completed by: _____

Position: _____

Date: _____

What is The Teaching and Learning Institute?

In 2005, after several months of prayer and dreaming, The Teaching and Learning Institute, legally known as TLI Inc., was born. TLI was created by public school administrators who collectively had over 50 years experience in the public school systems of New York State. We have served the children of the state in school districts ranging from small to large in rural, suburban and small city locations.

> **We have seen moral and ethical standards decline.**

During our careers we have also seen drastic changes in public education. Some changes have been less than desirable, other changes have certainly been for the good of all involved. Here are some examples of some of the changes we have seen.

We have seen state mandates and expectations for students increase dramatically and fortunately have seen students respond positively.

We have seen the costs of education skyrocket.

We have seen communities demand more and more of school districts and their personnel.

We have also seen less and less involvement and responsibility taken by parents.

We have seen moral and ethical standards decline.

We have seen more and more school boards lose sight of the reason they were created.

We have seen more and more school board members struggle to take over responsibilities which are not theirs to take.

TLI Inc. was created to help address many of these areas. Our mission statement and strategic plan outline our purposes and goals as well as the methods we are currently using to achieve them.

The Mission of The Teaching and Learning Institute is:

1) To increase the number of candidates who are willing to run for their local school board.
2) To identify teaching candidates who will champion high ethical standards and promote these standards throughout the entire employment process.

Candidates whether for the Board of Education or for teaching should be committed to family values based on a traditional Judeo-Christian belief system.

The Strategic Plan of The Teaching and Learning Institute is to:

- Develop awareness of the need for increased numbers of school board candidates who are committed to family values based on a traditional Judeo-Christian belief system.
- Provide regular television, radio and newspaper advertisements publicizing the opportunities available to people who are interested in becoming a candidate for their local school board or teacher candidates in the public school system.
- Make opinion pieces related to current educational issues available to newspapers on a periodic basis.
- Offer a variety of presentations to community groups interested in learning more about supporting traditional family values in our public schools.

- Offer training sessions to individuals who may be considering running for their local Board of Education.
- Encourage political leaders at the federal, state and local levels to support legislation that encourages family values based on a traditional Judeo-Christian belief system.
- Monitor proposed legislation in the New York and Pennsylvania State Legislature dealing with character education, moral issues, religion and ethics as it relates to PreK-12 education in the State and offer advice and counsel on these matters.
- Identify teaching candidates who will champion high ethical standards and promote these standards throughout the entire employment process.
- Conduct training session on writing a great resume and cover letter for individuals who may be considering a teaching career.
- Offer resume critique services and support to teacher candidates.

One of our major efforts to expand our influence and effort has been through the opportunity extended by the Family Life Radio Network (FLN) headquartered in Bath, NY. On the network we offer a Christian perspective on a wide variety of current public education issues in a weekly interview/discussion format. TLI is also frequently requested to offer commentary on various current issues in education that are mentioned on the news broadcasts on FLN. The Family Life Radio Network currently owns 14 stations and 52 translators. It engages a regular listening audience of 250,000 and has a potential audience to reach 4 million people daily throughout New York State and Pennsylvania.

As a direct result of this radio opportunity in 2007 we expanded our initial efforts in New York State into

Pennsylvania with its 501 school districts. From our conversations with Pennsylvania residents it appears that most of the issues of concern in New York State are also of concern in Pennsylvania.

In subsequent conversations with people from various parts of the country and from our research we have concluded that many of the issues initially recognized in New York State are the same educational issues and concerns throughout our country.

The Teaching and Learning Institute continues to look for practical ways to implement our Strategic Plan. This book, along with my previous book, The Sin of Apathy is part of that expanded effort. It was written with a very specific intention. That intention was to address the multitude of issues currently being faced by the public schools of our nation. Hopefully the book will be helpful in offering practical steps for parents, students, educators and also government and community leaders to make a positive impact on their local public schools.

The authors' desire is that **Many Options Few Easy Controlling School Spending** will also serve as an ongoing challenge of the need for citizen involvement in their local public school, particularly by people who are committed to family values based on a traditional Judeo-Christian belief system.

If you have been challenged in this way by these words I am eternally grateful and feel my work has been successful.

We are anxious to receive your comments, feedback and reaction to this book. We are also anxious to help you or other interested people to sort through the process of becoming a school board candidate.

For these or any other reasons we welcome your communication. The Teaching and Learning Institute (TLI Inc.) can be contacted in a variety of ways.

Website: www. teachingandlearninginstitute.org
Email: tli@frontiernet.net
Telephone: 585-567-2080
Mailing Address: P.O. Box 32, Houghton, NY 14744

TLI Inc. is a privately funded organization not affiliated with any other existing organization. We never ask for financial assistance from anyone who contacts us. All of our resources and materials are available at no cost to the recipients.